BRIDLINGTON
THROUGH TIME
Mike Hitches

AMBERLEY PUBLISHING

First published 2012

Amberley Publishing
The Hill, Stroud,
Gloucestershire, GL5 4EP

www.amberley-books.com

Copyright © Mike Hitches, 2012

The right of Mike Hitches to be identified as the
Author of this work has been asserted in accordance
with the Copyrights, Designs and Patents Act 1988.

ISBN 978 1 84868 255 9

British Library Cataloguing in Publication Data.
A catalogue record for this book is available from
the British Library.

Typeset in 9.5pt on 12pt Celeste.
Typesetting by Amberley Publishing.
Printed in the UK.

Introduction

Known through time as Bretlington, Brillinton, Breddelinton, Burlington and Bolliton by its natives, Bridlington and its surroundings have a long history. Roman roads and villas can be found nearby, and near Sewerby an Anglican cemetery marks the spot where Viking King Ida landed in AD 57. The harbour in Bridlington probably dates back to prehistoric times. Indeed, trade routes converged on the area from that period, as Irish gold was traded across the Pennines to Jutland, near modern Denmark, via Bridlington using existing roads, including Roman roads such as Woldgate. The priory dates back to medieval times and had its own harbour, at the mouth of the stream known as 'Gypsey Race'. The monastery at the priory had its own ships. One, the *Mariole*, is known to have exported locally-produced wool. After the dissolution of the monastery in 1537, stones from the priory were used to repair the harbour, its upkeep having now passed to the Lords Foeffes of Bridlington Manor. Any proposed changes there would henceforth have been subject to an Act of Parliament.

The priory was granted the right to hold a market and fair in 1200. High Green was the location for the fair, and may well have hosted the market before it was moved to Market Place at the far end of Old Town. Old Town itself probably dates back to the establishment of the priory. Nowadays it is more famous for its narrow streets and the Georgian façades of its buildings. Some of these frontages also contain priory stone taken after the monastery's dissolution and destruction in Henry VIII's reign. Old Town and the more modern Bridlington, established around the Quay and harbour were separate for some time, Old Town being the business and trading centre, while the area around the Quay was largely involved in fishing, along with the import and export of goods. Some 300 fishing boats were using the harbour in 1902, 84 of which were Bridlington-based. The Scottish fishing fleet would often call at the harbour, with as many as 100 vessels at the port on August Sundays.

The linking of the Old Town and the Quay came about due to the expansion of Bridlington as a holiday resort thanks to the arrival of the railway in the town. A line opened from Hull in 1846 and the extension from Filey and Scarborough was completed the following year. Prior to the opening of the railway, arrival in Bridlington was primarily by stagecoach. The *British Queen* took four hours from Hull using the coast road; it terminated at Stirling Castle Inn on the Quay. Another coach, the *Wellington*, took the high road along the edge of the Wolds, via Driffield, and arrived at the Cross Keys Inn in Old Town. When the railway finally reached Bridlington, the railway station was built about halfway between the resort area around the Quay and the business district of Old Town, which position has always been inconvenient for holidaymakers and thus favours modern travel by motor coach or car. This rather odd location of the station is down to the residents of Old Town. They objected to the railway running down to the Quay, which was much more sparsely populated, having only 1,000 inhabitants, compared to 4,000 in Old Town. They also pointed out that Old Town was the centre of trade and manufacturing, while the Quay was primarily for pleasure.

Following the opening of the railway, Bridlington expanded rapidly, and Old Town and the Quay became linked by buildings along Quay Road. After the 1860s, large-scale building began between the Promenade and the seafront, mainly of four-storey lodging houses. Inland estates followed in the 1870s, but by far the biggest expansion occurred between 1881 and 1901, with considerable building in Hilderthorpe. Indeed, the population of the borough of Bridlington increased from 6,480 in 1891 to 12,482 a decade later. To cater for the demands of holidaymakers, attractions were built, including the Victoria Rooms on the North Pier in 1846, the New Spa (which was burnt down several times) and the People's Palace in 1896, the Hydro on South Marine Drive in 1898, and the Floral Hall in 1904.

From these nineteenth- and twentieth-century developments, Bridlington became the seaside town and resort known today. In recent times, like many such resorts, it has suffered from the loss of tourists as package holidays to sunnier climes become cheaper and more attractive. However, increasing fuel costs and currency fluctuations, not to mention a reduction in disposable income due to wage freezes and rising prices, have made holidays abroad more expensive; this may have the effect of bringing tourists back into the town and, it is hoped, will bring new prosperity to this famous east-coast resort.

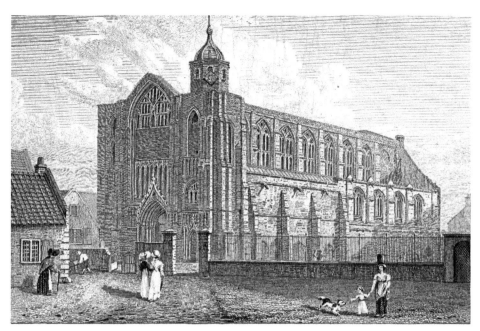

The Priory Church

The old priory church, built on land that had been given to Gilbert de Gant in 1072, a nephew of King Stephen. His eldest son, Walter de Gant, founded an Augustinian priory on the land in 1133. A charter by Henry I confirmed the role of the priory. Successive kings extended the priory over the years. Along with land, King John granted the right to hold a weekly market and annual fair in 1200. Later, Henry VI allowed the priory to hold three annual fairs, and it was from this point that the town grew up around the priory. Below is the priory, now the church of St Mary following the dissolution of the monasteries under King Henry VIII.

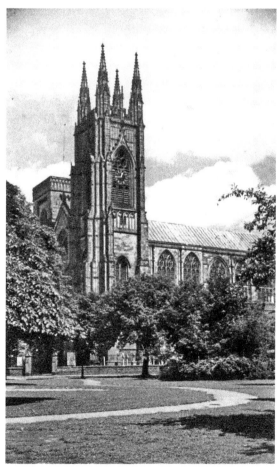

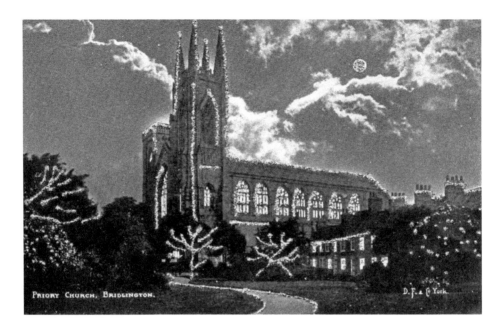

Priory Church, Bridlington. D.F. & Co York

The Priory at Night
The upper view shows the priory at night, while the lower view shows it in daylight, March 2012. Even before the markets were established, King Stephen gave the priory the right to have a port, which the monks put to good use. Bridlington had its own saint, St John of Bridlington (1320–1379), who was one of the last English saints to be canonised, in 1401, before the Reformation. His shrine has attracted many worshippers, including at least two monarchs: Henry IV and Henry V.

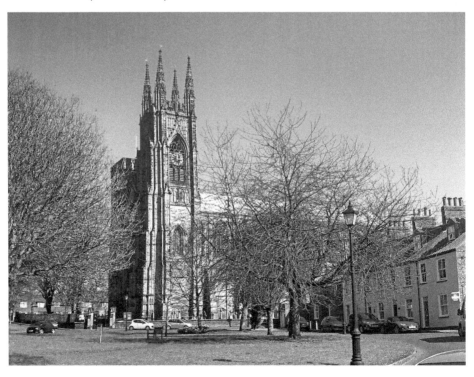

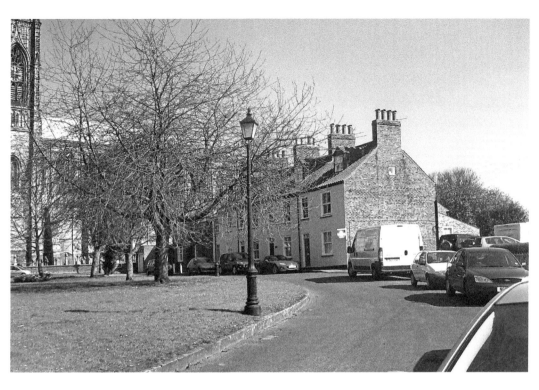

Church Green
Cottages and houses in Church Green in March 2012, giving an impression of the calm and peaceful area around the church.

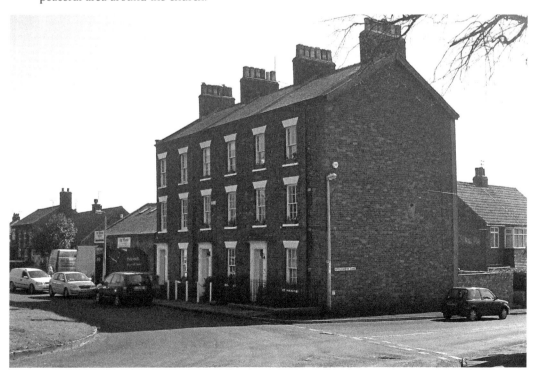

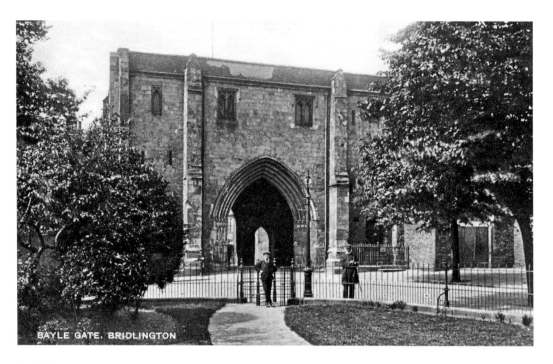

BAYLE GATE. BRIDLINGTON

Bayle Gate

Two views of Bayle Gate. The upper photograph was taken in the 1930s when the road passed through the gate. Below is the Gate in 2012, the road bypassing it. The Bayle dates back to 1388, and was the gatehouse to the priory. Later it became the prison and manor courtroom, held in trust by the Lords Feoffes, who still meet here. The Bayle is now a museum.

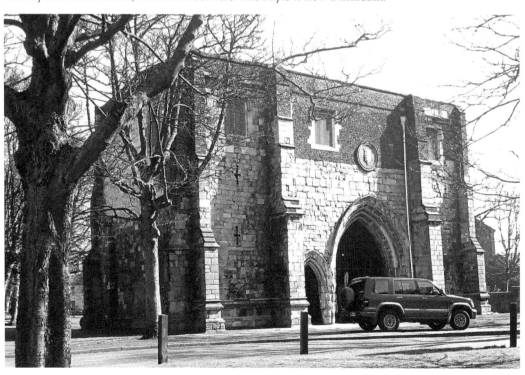

The Lords Foeffes

Bayle Gate in the eighteenth century, at a time when cottages were situated on the road leading to Bayle. After the dissolution, the Manor of Bridlington remained the property of the Crown until 1624, when Charles I granted it to Sir John Ramsay, Earl of Holderness. In 1633 he sold the Manor to thirteen inhabitants of the town on behalf of the tenants of the Manor. By May 1636, a deed was drawn up that empowered the thirteen men as Lords Foeffes (trust holders) of the Manor of Bridlington. The lower view shows Kirkgate looking towards the priory in the late nineteenth century, these cottages having replaced those close to the Bayle.

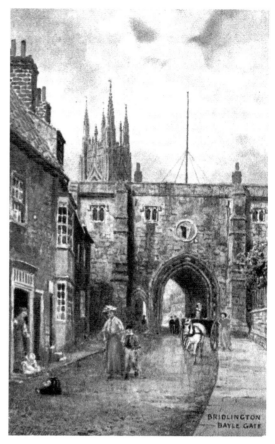

BRIDLINGTON
BAYLE GATE

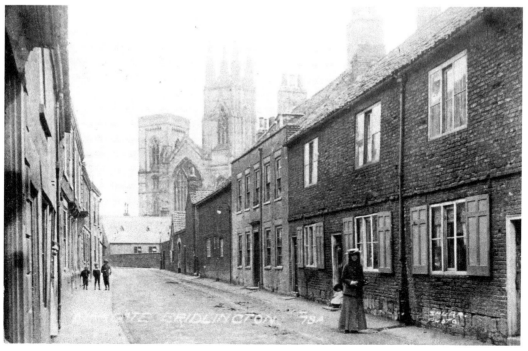

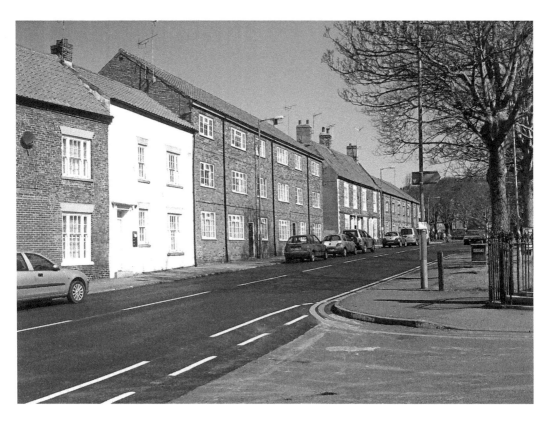

Kirkgate

The upper view shows modern Kirkgate, its cottages appear well-preserved. Below is the narrow High Street in Old Town, with its Georgian buildings, many of which were built using stone taken from the old monastery after it was dissolved.

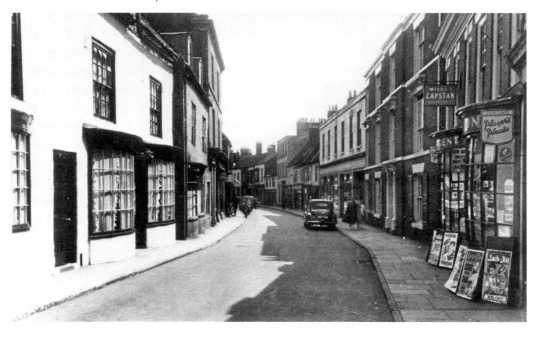

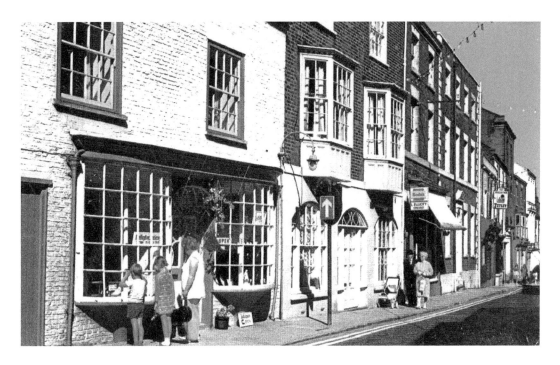

Old Town

Old Town in the 1950s and on 11 December 2011, the latter taken during the Dickensian Festival. Old Town is the original part of Bridlington and was known as Burlington for many years. Indeed, the first newspaper in the town was called the *Burlington Reporter*.

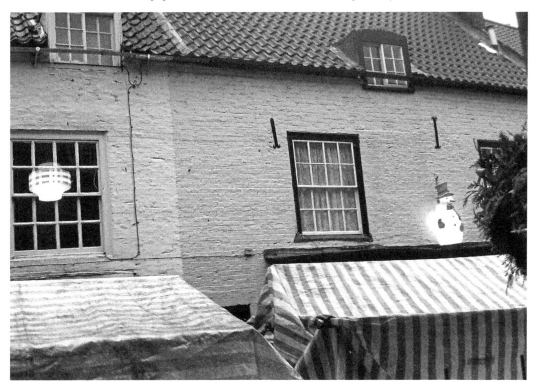

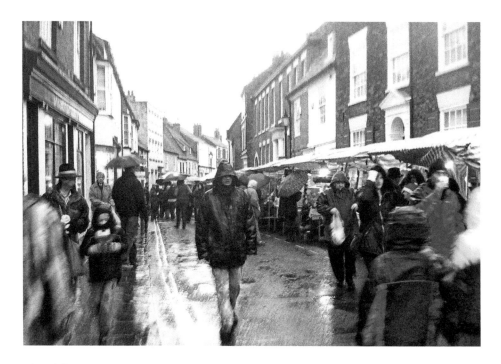

The Dickensian Festival

High Street in Old Town on 11 December 2011, with the Dickensian Festival in full swing. The festival occurs every year on one Sunday around Christmas time, and is always well attended, whatever the weather – on this particular occasion, heavy rainfall. The shops and cottages on the High Street are decorated specially for the event and stalls and fairground rides fill the road outside. A brass band plays all afternoon to provide musical entertainment.

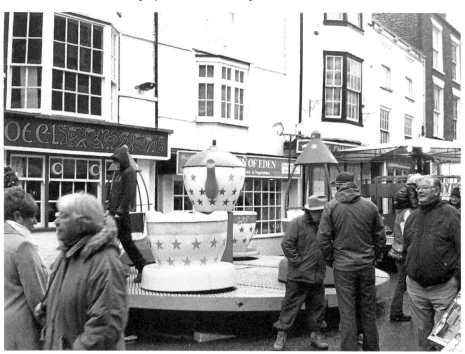

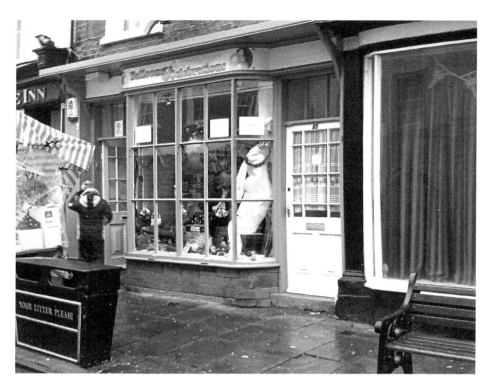

High Street

Shops on High Street, which have been decorated for the event. Some beautiful Georgian architecture is also visible here. The rear of High street is shown in the lower view.

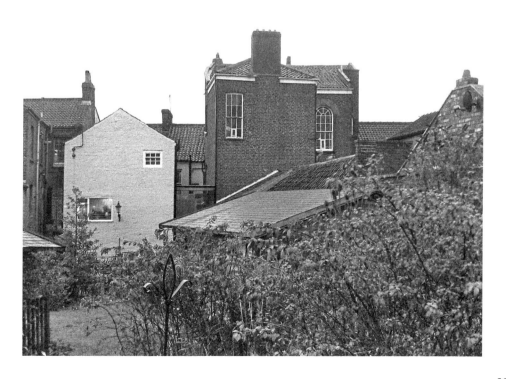

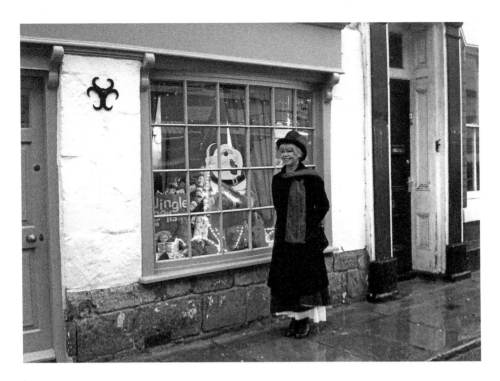

Victorian Bridlington

Standing outside one of the High Street shops is Tina Pickering, dressed in Victorian costume to give further atmosphere to the day. Below, local historian David Mooney is dressed as a policeman of the period. It was not until 1823 that Bridlington acquired its first policeman, when the population of the town began to reach some 4,000 souls.

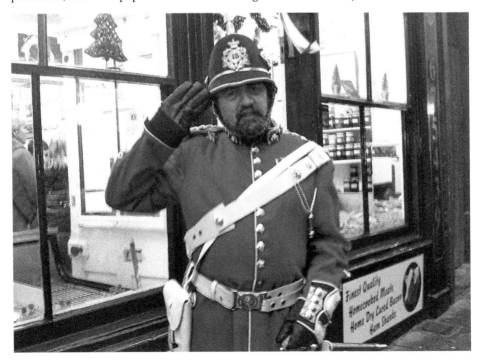

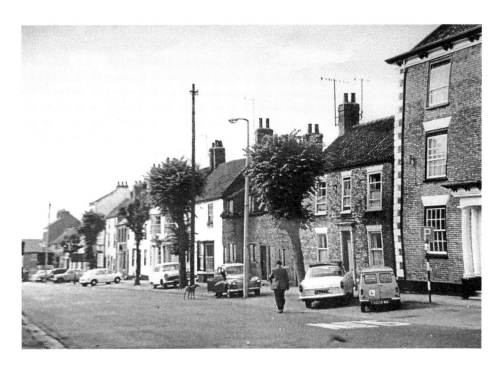

Market Place

Market Place, seen here in the 1960s, was once known as Cross Hill. It was the site of the old market and contains many old buildings. At the junction of the Scarborough Road, on the right, is a flower shop that was once the stables of the horses for the local hunt. Below is The Packhorse on Market Place in the late nineteenth century. A relic of the medieval period, in the form of the town stocks, is situated outside the Packhorse, although they are not visible in this view.

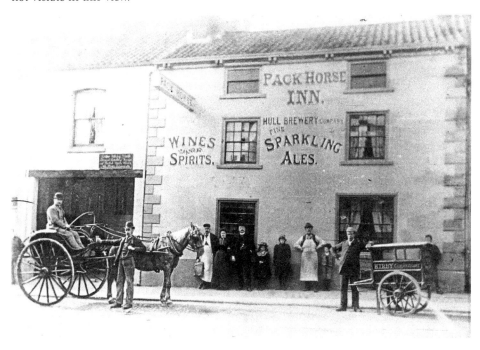

15

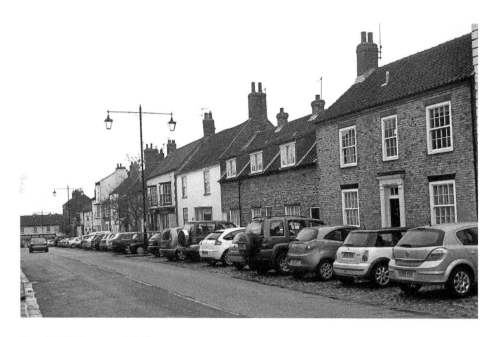

Notable Visitors to Bridlington

Market Place in December 2011, showing the well-preserved buildings here. There were several important visitors to Old Town who would have recognised some of these buildings, including Queen Henrietta Maria, wife of Charles I. She landed at Bridlington in February 1643, during the Civil War, to the sound of gunfire from Parliamentarian ships, before making her way to York where she established her headquarters. Another Royal visitor was Prince William Henry, later William IV, who landed in July 1785. He stayed at the Ship Inn, later the Britannia Hotel. Charlotte Brontë first visited Bridlington in 1839, travelling by rail from Leeds to Selby and reaching the town by road coach; the railway would not reach the town for almost another decade.

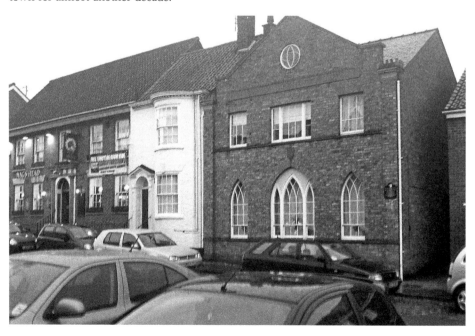

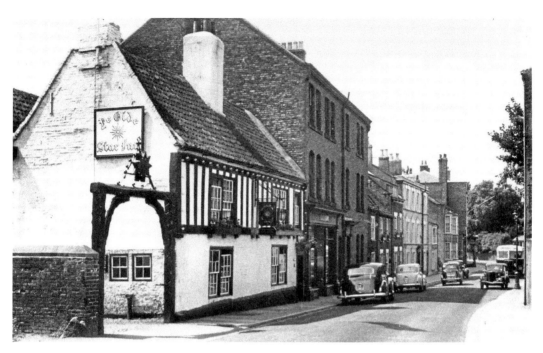

Ye Old Star Inn

Above is a view of Ye Old Star Inn in the 1950s. The public house has been here for many years and is part of the character of the Old Town. There is even the suggestion that the inn is haunted, as many of the buildings in Old Town are believed to be. Below, Tina Pickering is pictured leaving the inn in December 2011.

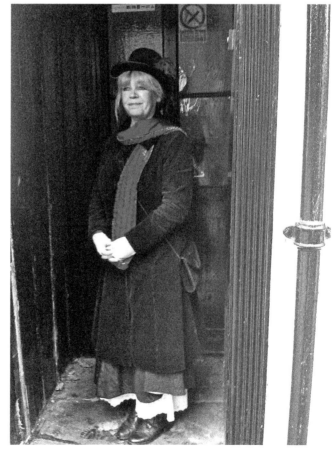

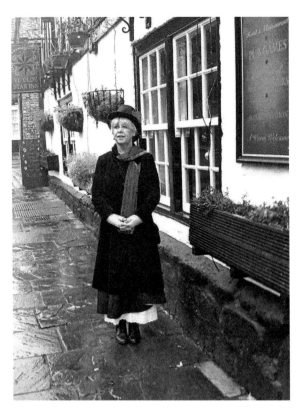

The Middleton Hunt
Tina is again seen here at Ye Old Star Inn and on the step outside, which ladies would use to mount their horses for the hunt. The Middleton Hunt was centred here for several years.

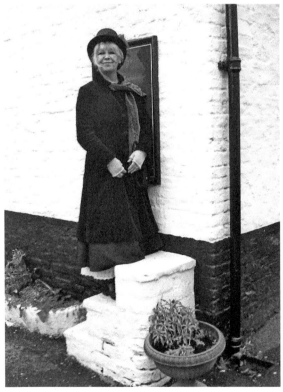

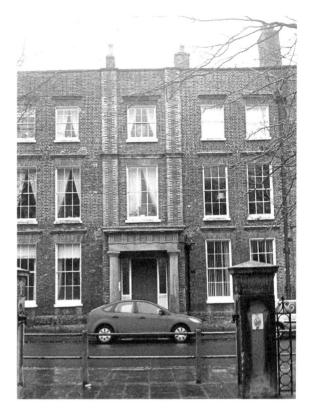

The Avenue
Two views of The Avenue in Old Town. The Avenue was built for the Pickett family in 1714 and was bought by Thomas Pickett in 1760. In 1932, the Avenue became a hospital. However, when Bridlington District Hospital later opened, it was left derelict. It has since become a listed building and was converted into apartments in 1993.

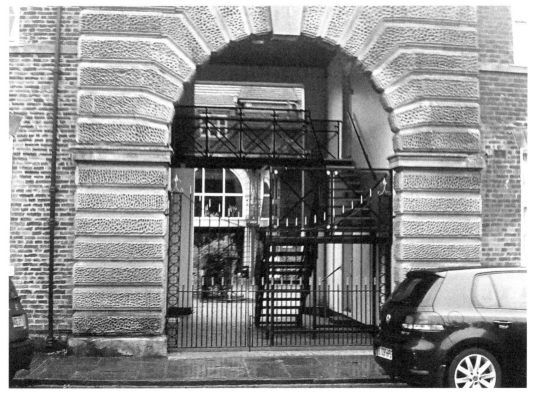

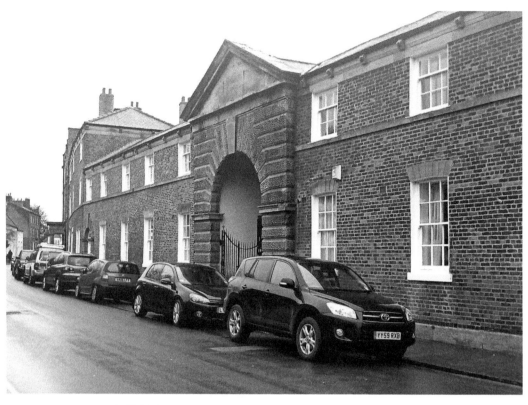

Avenue Hospital

Above is the former maternity unit at Avenue Hospital, which was transferred to the new hospital when it opened. Below, two midwives pose outside the Avenue maternity unit in the early 1960s.

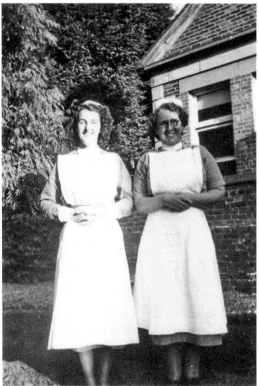

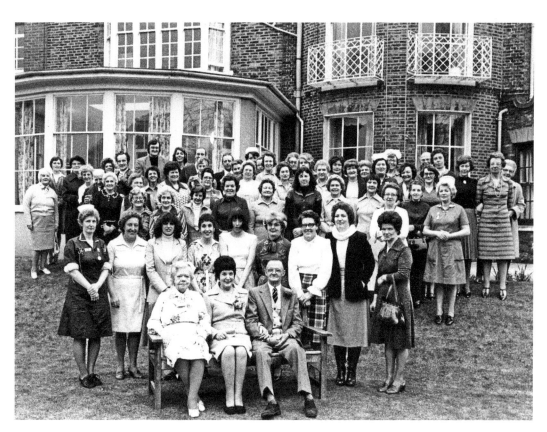

Avenue Maternity Unit
Midwives and nursing staff at Avenue Maternity Unit in the early 1970s, posing in a Nativity scene. In view are Midwife Sister Brigham with SEN Mary Walker below. Two unnamed nurses are on the left of the scene. Above, staff at Avenue Hospital pose in the grounds behind the hospital at the retirement of Dr Wilson.

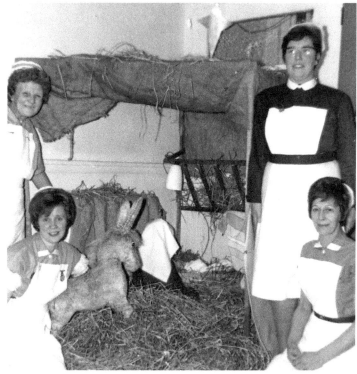

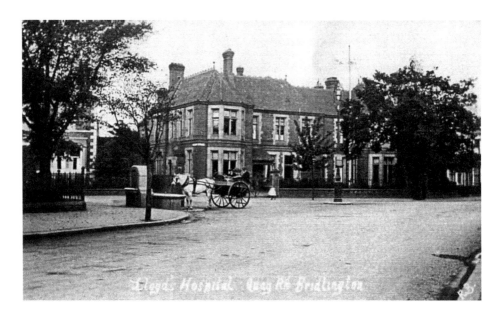

Lloyd Hospital

A view of Lloyd Hospital at the end of the nineteenth century. Alicia Marie Lloyd presented £1,200 to the town to found a dispensary in the town. Although local doctors opposed the establishment, because they thought people would prefer to receive free treatment there rather than pay them, the hospital was opened in Quay Road in 1868 and extended in 1875. Plans for a new building were drawn up, with an estimated cost of £1,800, and a plot was purchased on Medina Avenue. This new hospital opened in April 1876 at a total cost of £32,200, which included the building, fixtures and fittings and fifteen beds. The hospital closed in 1988 when the new District Hospital opened. Lloyd Hospital was put up for sale, and was eventually demolished. A Mormon church is now on the site, as this 2012 view shows.

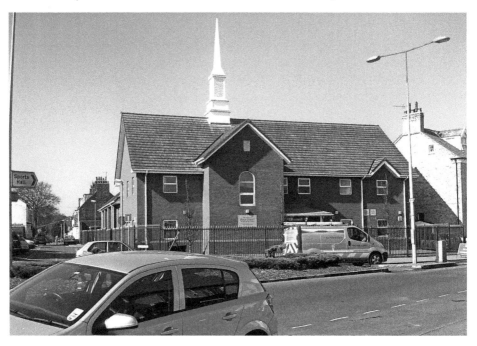

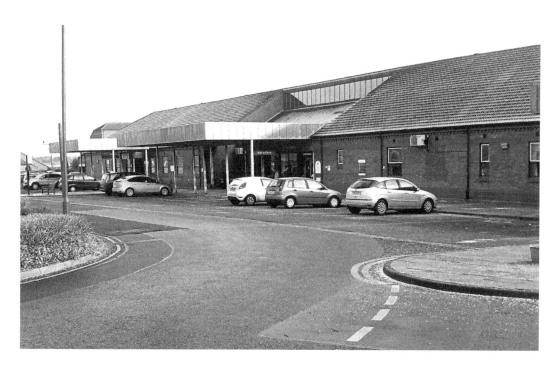

Bridlington District Hospital

Bridlington District Hospital opened in 10 March 1988 and cost £16 million to build. On its opening, patients were moved from the Avenue, Lloyds and Bempton Lane Hospitals, the old buildings being put up for sale. Lloyd and Avenue Hospitals were sold on 8 December 1988. Bempton Lane Isolation Hospital was eventually demolished and a housing estate was built on the site. The first baby born at the new hospital was a boy, Richard Cottey, and the first girl was Louise Sabin. Both arrived on the same day – 10 March 1988.

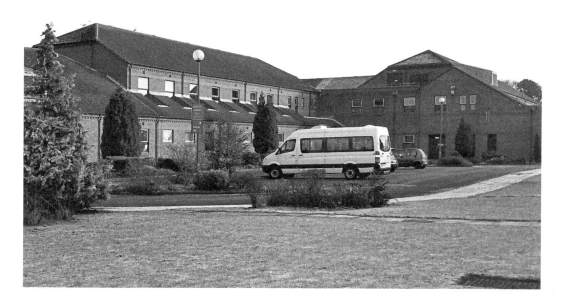

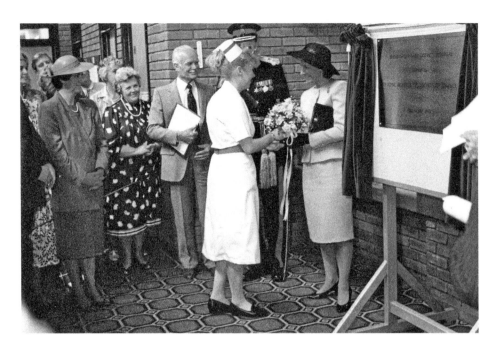

A Royal Occasion

Although the new Bridlington Hospital had been opened in March 1988, its official opening did not take place until 16 May 1989. The hospital management had hoped to make it a Royal occasion, and the Duchess of Gloucester had accepted an invitation to preside over the occasion, but could only do so in May the following year, hence the delay. Here, on 16 May, the Duchess is seen being presented with a bouquet by a member of nursing staff after unveiling the plaque commemorating the official opening of the hospital. Afterwards she toured the hospital, and is seen being welcomed at the entrance of one of the wards by the ward sister.

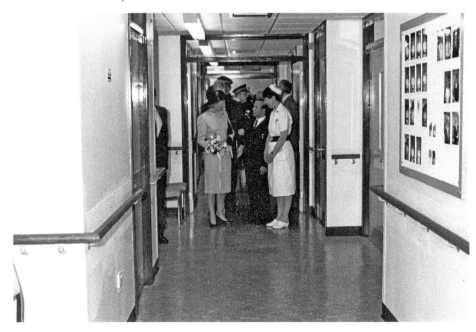

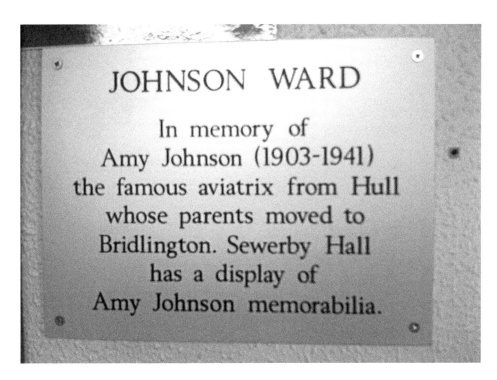

Johnson Ward, Bridlington District Hospital

At the entrance to Johnson Ward, a plaque commemorates Amy Johnson, the famous aviatrix from Hull. Below are members of the nursing staff on Johnson Ward on Christmas Day 2011. From left to right are: Judith Lea, Helen Kelly (appropriately decorated for the occasion), Margaret Parris and Tina Pickering. In front is ward manager, Sister Carol 'Mary' Jagger.

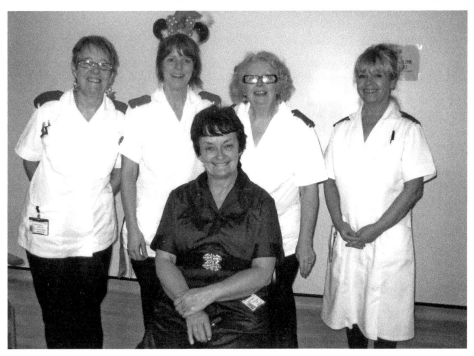

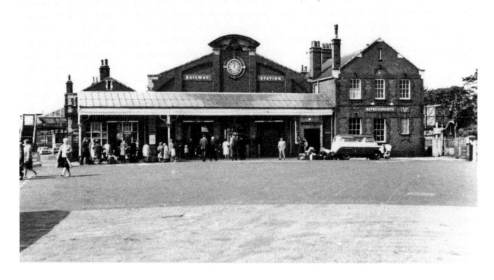

Railway Station

The exterior of Bridlington railway station in August 1967 and February 2012. A railway that would have linked the seaside town to West Yorkshire was suggested as early as 1834, when a line was projected to run from Bridlington Quay to join the Leeds and Selby railway, but nothing came of it. However, by 1845/46 railways approached Bridlington from both Hull and Scarborough. The Hull & Selby Railway promoted the line from Hull to Bridlington, while George Hudson's York & North Midland Railway promoted a line from Seamer, where it would leave the main York–Scarborough railway, the two lines making a head-on connection at Bridlington. Both were authorised on 30 June 1845. The following year, on 6 October, the line from Hull was opened, to be followed by the line from Seamer a year later.

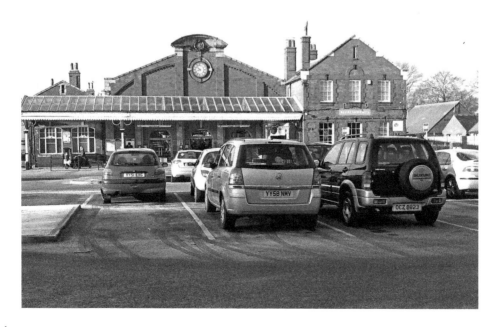

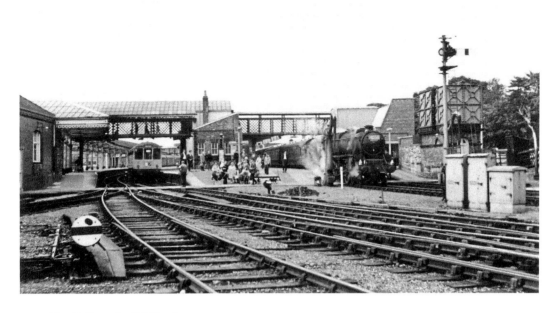

The Railway in Bridlington

Bridlington railway station in August 1967 and February 2012. The upper view shows an excursion train awaiting departure for the West Riding, headed by ex-LMS Black Five 4-6-0 no. 44694 (a foreign loco in the town) with a diesel multiple-unit train on a local service from Scarborough to Hull. The lower view shows a pair of Class 158 Sprinter two-coach trains; the one on the left is for Scarborough and the one on the right is for Hull. In the 'boom' railway years of the 1950s and '60s, Bridlington could be very busy with excursion trains during the summer months, which brought much income to the local economy.

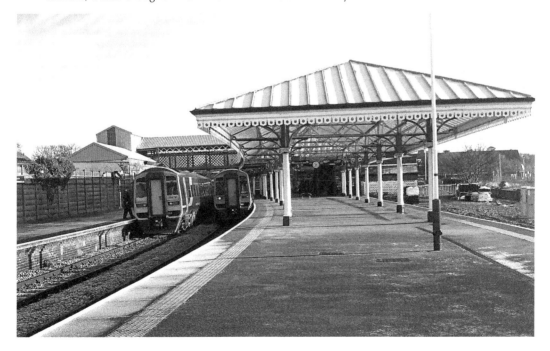

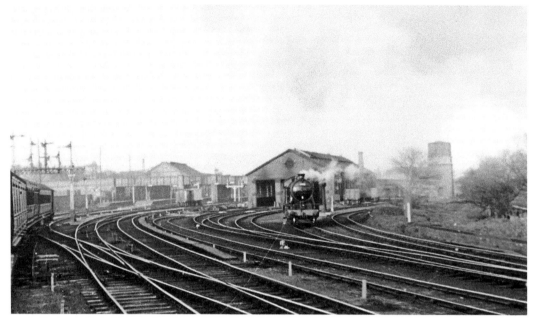

Bridlington Locoshed

The upper view shows Bridlington locoshed looking towards the station in April 1953, with an ex-LNER steam loco awaiting its turn of duty. A locoshed here had almost certainly existed when the line from Hull opened in 1846. A new shed, however, was constructed in 1892 and was to last until it closed in 1958, being finally abandoned in October 1968. As can be seen in the lower 2012 view, looking towards Hull from the station platform, a B&Q DIY store now occupies the site.

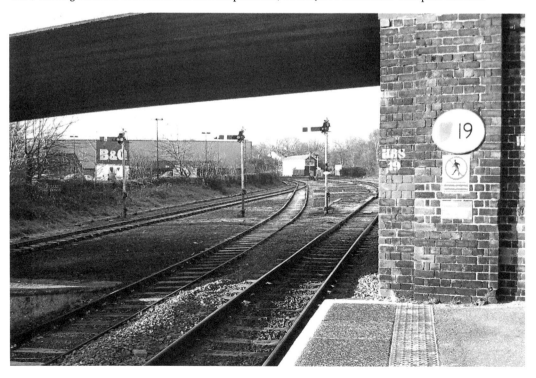

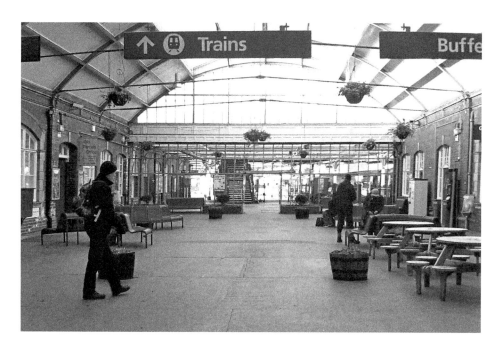

The Grand Opening

The concourse and ticket office at Bridlington station in February 2012. The spacious area here contains large displays of flowers during the summer months, looked after by the staff. The concourse retains much of its former elegance, giving a hint of the high-class visitors who came to Bridlington during the Victorian and Edwardian periods. When the railway was opened, the ceremony was a great event, with sixty carriages hauled by three locomotives arriving in the town. Two brass bands played to welcome visitors and 2,000 people arrived for the event.

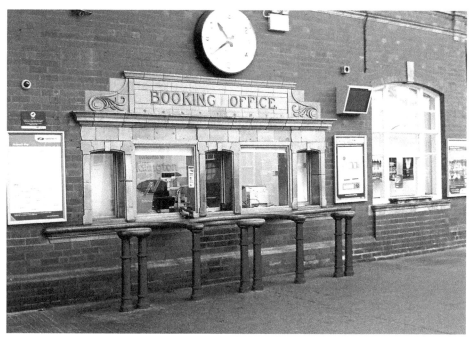

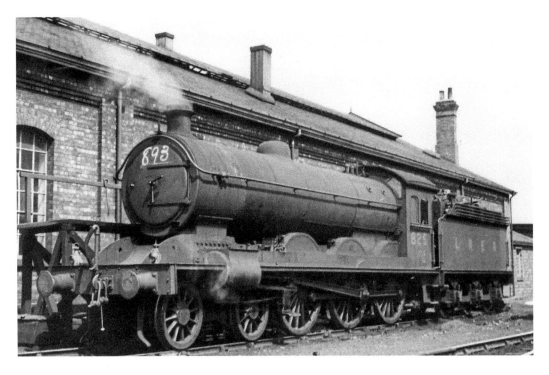

Trains at Bridlington

Standing outside Bridlington locoshed is ex-North Eastern railway 4-6-0 in LNER livery no. 825. Awaiting departure from Bridlington station on 6 March 1965 is an excursion train headed by K4 2-6-0 no. 3442 *The Great Marquess* in LNER apple-green livery, and ex-LNER K1 2-6-0 no. 62005 in British Railways black livery.

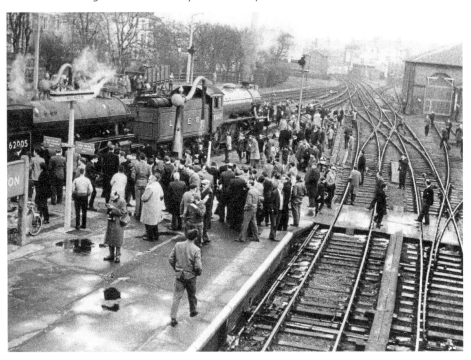

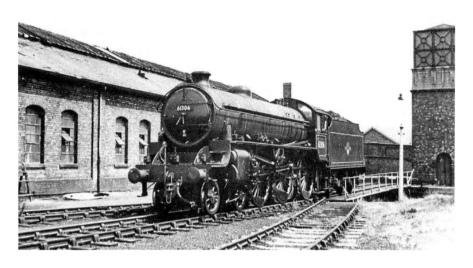

Trains at Bridlington

The upper view shows Thompson B1 4-6-0 no. 61336 arriving at Bridlington station. The building on the left now contains The Bed Warehouse. Below, in 1958, ex-LNER V3 class 2-6-0 tank loco is at the head of a local service to Hull, seen passing the Bridlington south signal box.

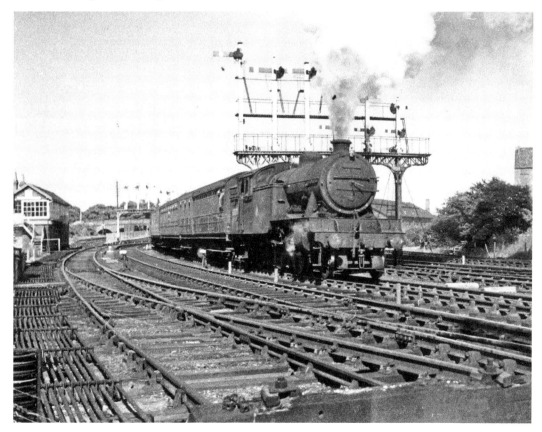

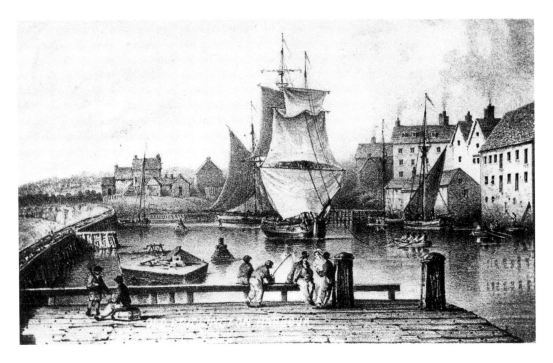

Bridlington Quay

The harbour at Bridlington in the eighteenth century, with a sailing ship rigged and ready to leave. A small fishing port grew up here from the very early days and the area developed and became known as Bridlington Quay. It was only the discovery of a chalybeate spring that allowed nineteenth-century development here. There is clearly very little development in this upper view. The lower view shows the end of the harbour in the nineteenth century, with a steam tug pulling a sailing boat into the harbour. As can be seen, there has been much building work around the harbour to accommodate the increasing number of visitors, many brought in by the new railway.

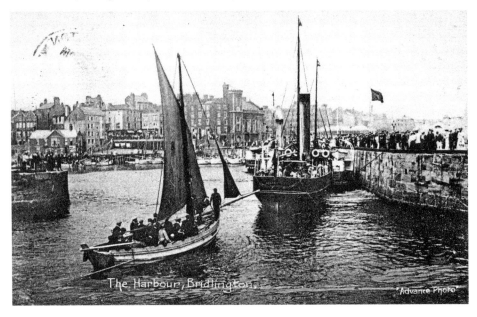

The Harbour, Bridlington.

'Advance Photo'

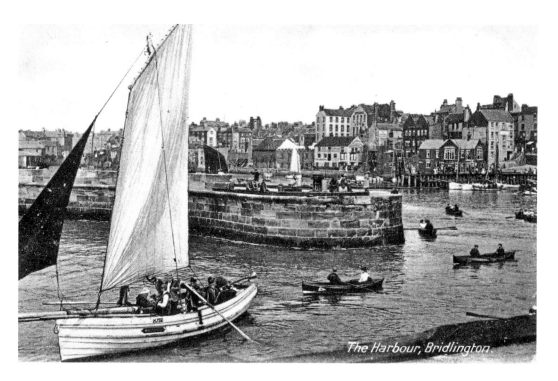

The Harbour, Bridlington.

The Harbour Wall and Piers

Two further views of the harbour and the harbour wall. By the seventeenth century, trade had developed, with exports of corn, malt, barley and Bridlington beer. Trade to the Baltic was also important and harbour improvements had to be made. In the early nineteenth century, John Rennie surveyed the harbour and in 1816 work began on new stone piers. By 1848, both the north and south piers had been constructed.

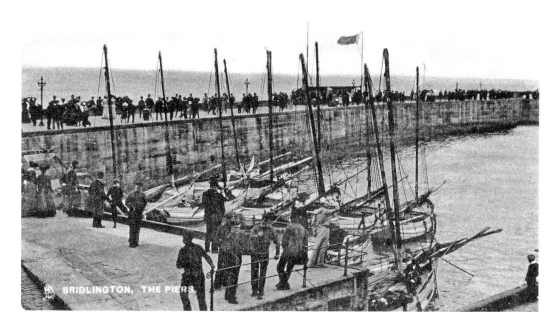

BRIDLINGTON. THE PIERS.

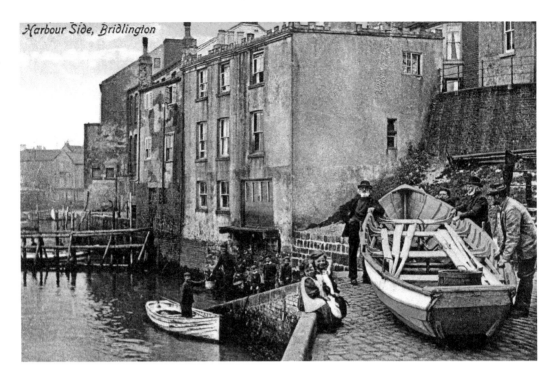

Harbour Side, Bridlington

The Harbour

Nineteenth- and early twentieth-century views of Bridlington harbour, the lower view showing how popular this location was with visitors, who at this time would enjoy watching the goings-on here. In the early years, smuggling was a common practice in Bridlington, as it was elsewhere along the coast, and secret passages were said to exist under the pier end of Garrison Street.

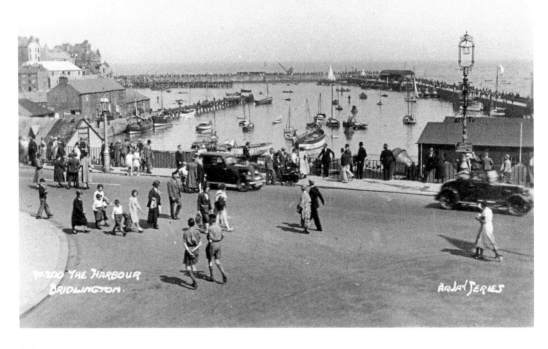

THE HARBOUR BRIDLINGTON.

ARJAY SERIES

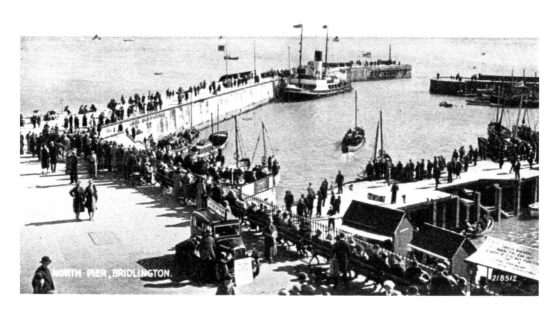

Sea Bathing

General views of Bridlington Quay during the summer season. By the 1760s sea trade began to decline at the Quay. On the other hand, the fashion for sea bathing emerged from the 1730s and the Quay was attracting visitors for this purpose by 1770, which compensated somewhat for the loss of sea trade. However, the main market area was in Old Town and even as late as 1780 it was virtually impossible to purchase anything at the Quay.

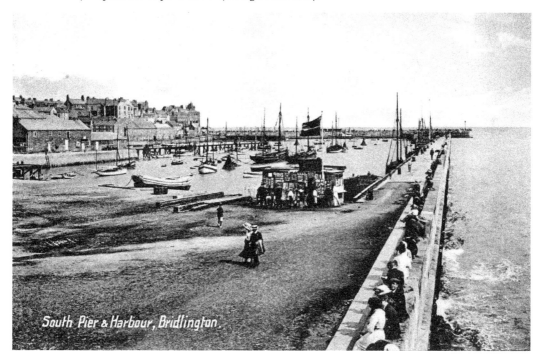

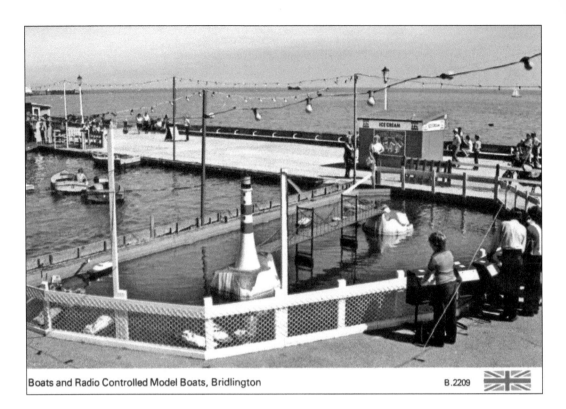

Boats and Radio Controlled Model Boats, Bridlington   B.2209

The 1950s Harbour and Quay
A further view of the harbour and Quay in the 1950s.

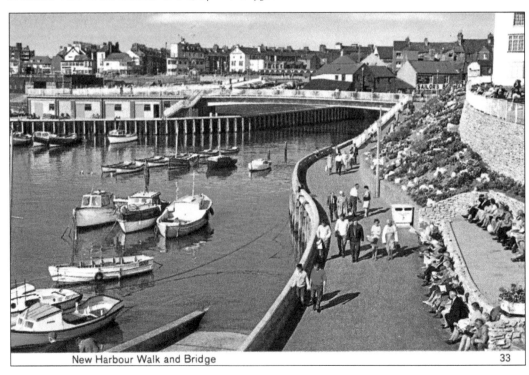

New Harbour Walk and Bridge   33

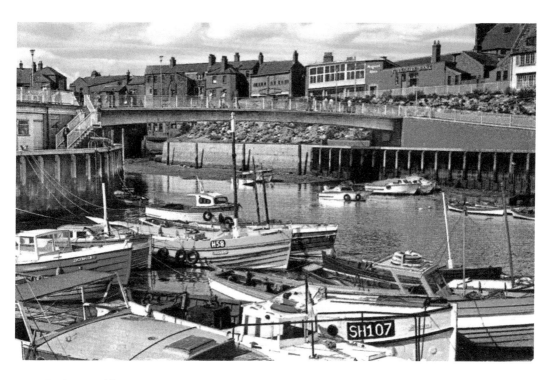

Harbour Bridge

The upper view shows the old harbour bridge, which was demolished in 1996 when the High Street was refurbished. Below you cna see the harbour wall in May 2006 with a pleasure craft alongside.

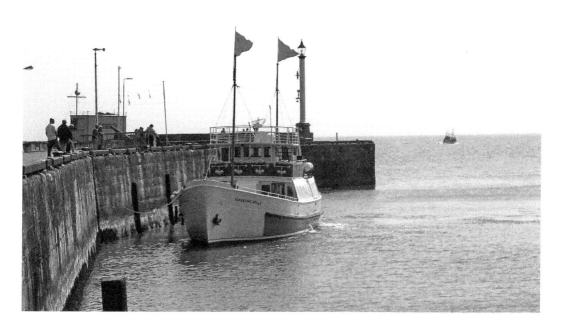

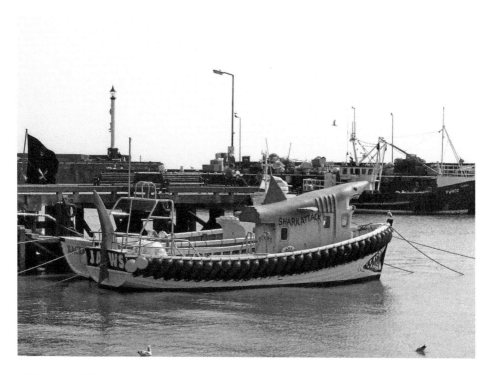

Fishing in Bridlington

Pleasure boats can be seen at the harbour in May 2006 after the area was renovated and is used for pleasure craft as well as fishing cobles. Indeed, the harbour here still has a lucrative export market of shellfish to mainland Europe worth several million pounds to the local economy.

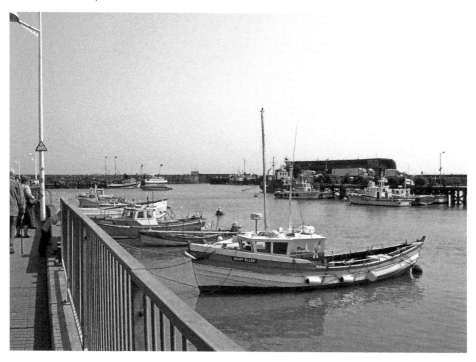

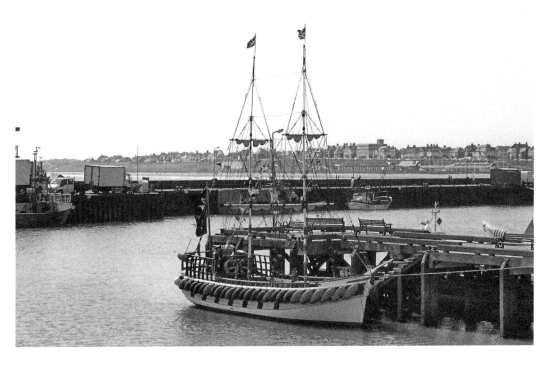

Pirate Ship and Fishing Cobles

Further views of the harbour in 2006. The upper picture shows the 'pirate ship', which offers a short tour around the harbour area during the holiday season. The lower view shows the end of the harbour wall, with fishing cobles unloading their catch.

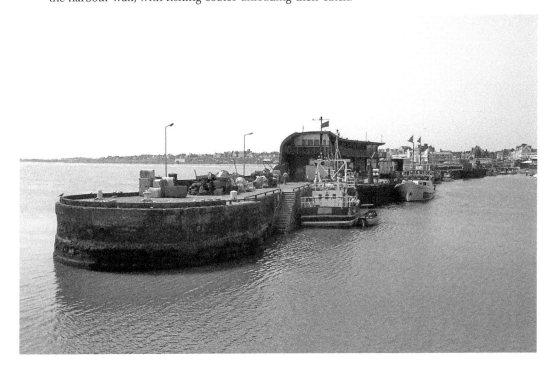

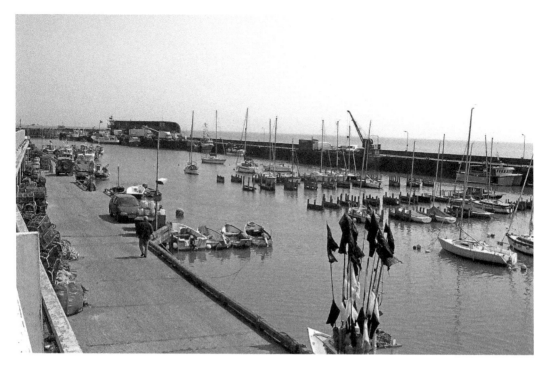

The Great Gale

Further views of the harbour and marina in May 2006. The worst sea disaster at Bridlington occurred on 10 February 1871, when the Great Gale drove some thirty ships on shore and more than seventy men were lost, including six lifeboatmen from the *Harbinger*, which capsized. Remembrance services were held for them at the priory for a century.

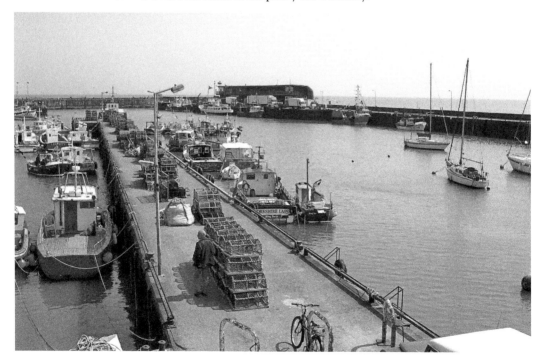

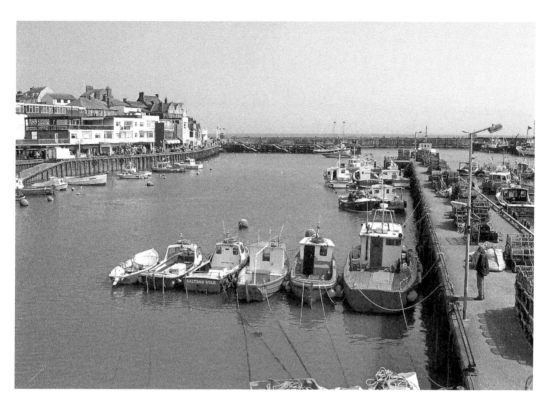

Marina and Seashore
The harbour marina and seashore captured in May 2006.

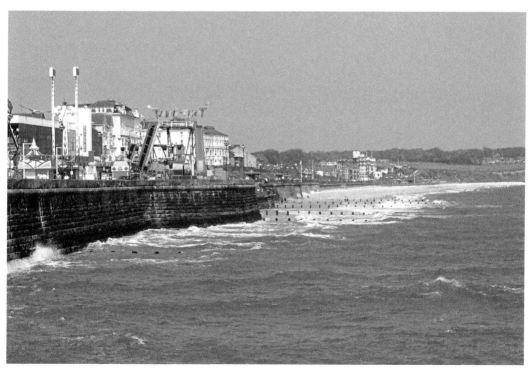

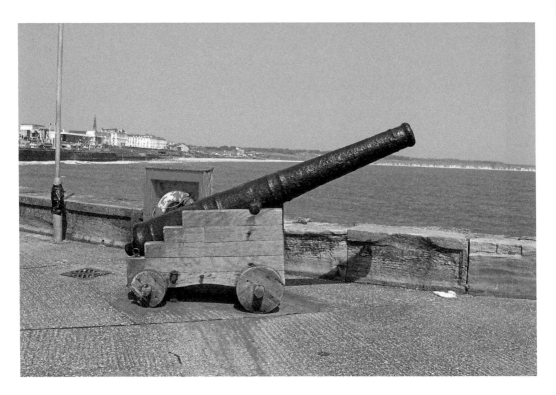

Harbour Cannon

Further views of the harbour wall in 2006, the upper view showing the cannon that guards the harbour. It was most likely positioned here in reaction to an attack by Dutch boats in 1666. The following year a fort was built next to the sea, where Leisure World now stands. Below, the harbour wall is seen from across the Quay.

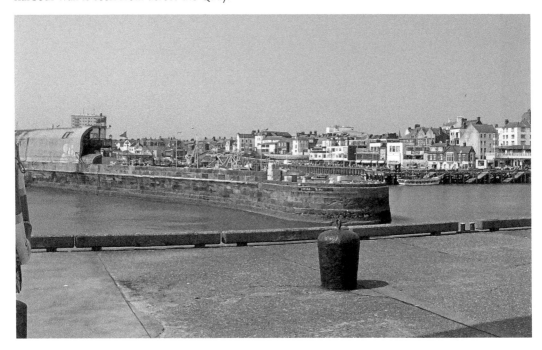

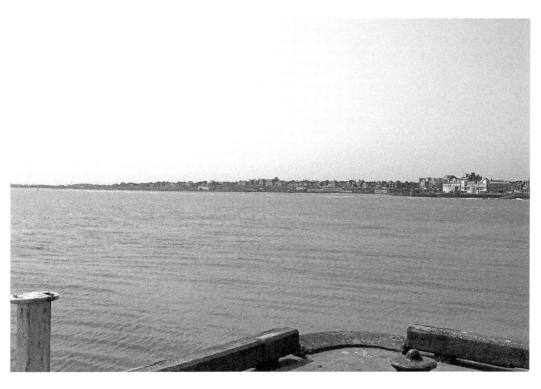

Seascapes
Seascapes at Bridlington in May 2006 and some forty years earlier.

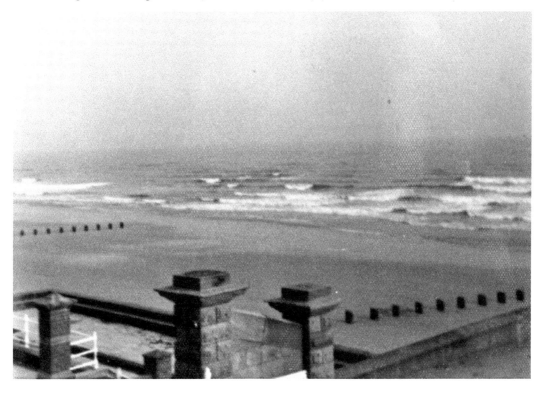

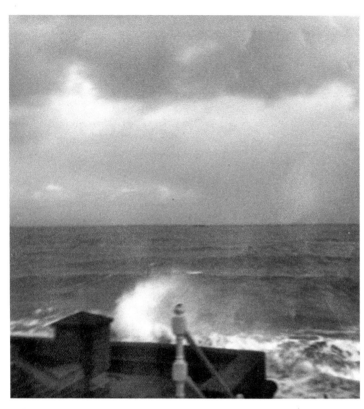

Storms over Bridlington
Stormy seas and grey skies at Bridlington in the 1970s. The lower view shows Flamborough cliffs in the background.

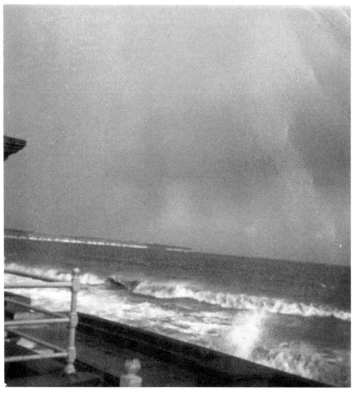

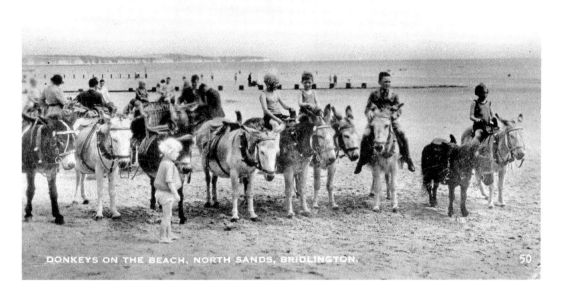

DONKEYS ON THE BEACH, NORTH SANDS, BRIDLINGTON. 50

Donkeys

Donkeys on the beach were introduced at Bridlington in 1896. Donkey rides have long been associated with seaside holidays and have always been popular with children, as can be seen here. Below is a general view of the south side, with its Promenade and sea walls. The sea walls were built in 1870s as part of a drainage improvement scheme. The parade and sea wall were opened by Prince Albert Victor in 1888.

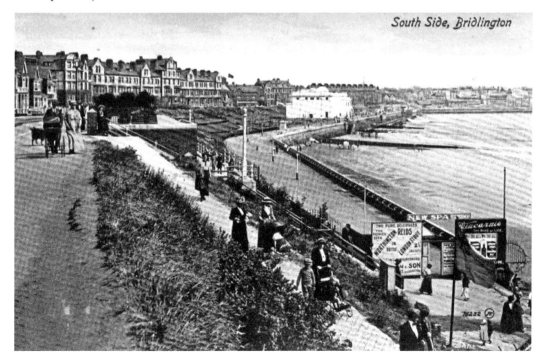

South Side, Bridlington

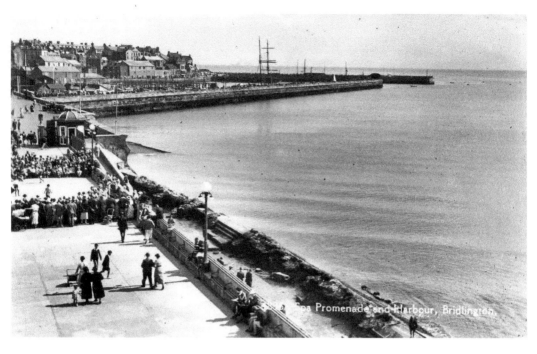

Spa Promenade and Harbour, Bridlington.

South Side

The south side shore in the early twentieth and twenty-first centuries, with the harbour in view in the background.

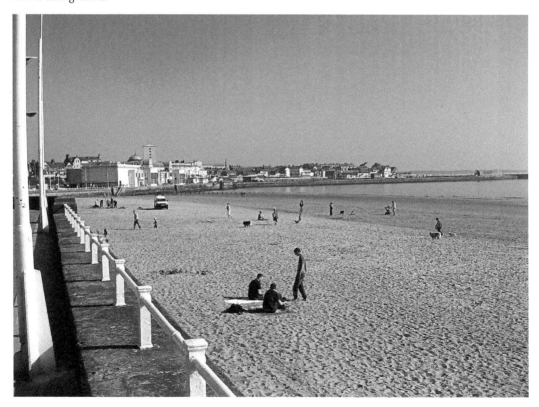

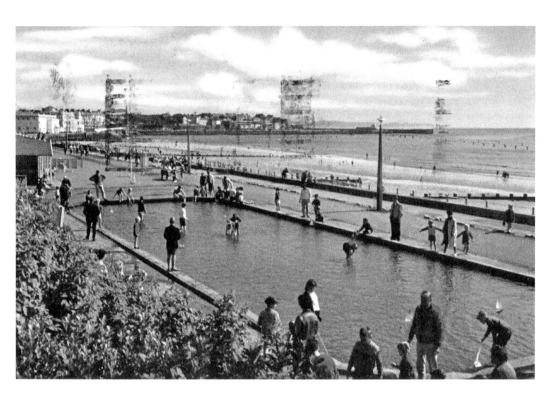

Boating and Paddling
South Bay and Promenade showing the boating pool (above) at the height of the summer season, with a busy beach and sea. The quieter 1960s lower view shows the paddling pool.

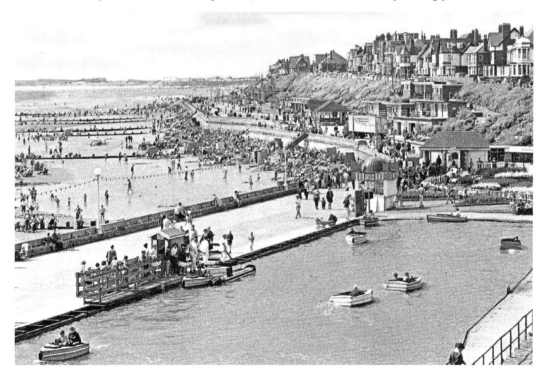

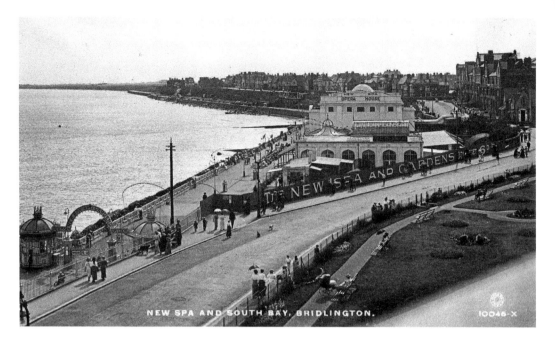

South Side Development

The upper view shows New Spa and South Bay in the 1930s. The lower view shows the Royal Hall and Promenade packed with visitors. Development of the south side began in 1894 when the Spa and Garden Company started their building work here. The first spa building was destroyed by fire in 1906 and rebuilt the following year. It was extended between 1925 and 1928. This building was also destroyed by fire, and it was rebuilt in its current art deco style in 1932. The Royal Hall was reputed to have the largest dancefloor in the north of England and also housed the theatre.

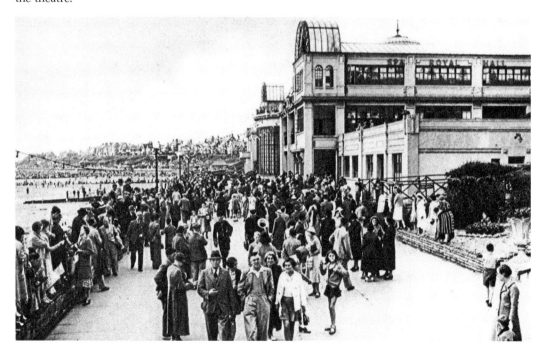

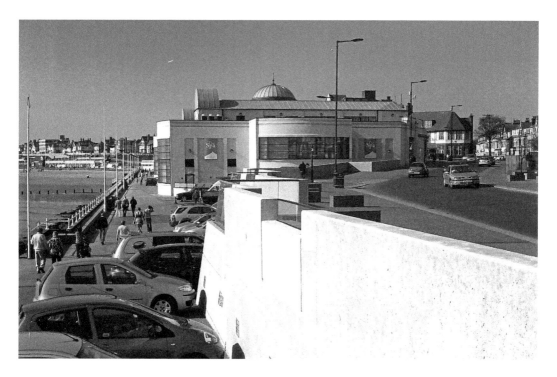

New Spa

New Spa as it appeared in March 2012, showing its art deco architecture. The spa is now under the control of East Yorkshire County Council and hosts theatrical and musical events as well as private functions. In the 1990s improvements were made to the Spa Promenade and it was reopened in 1996.

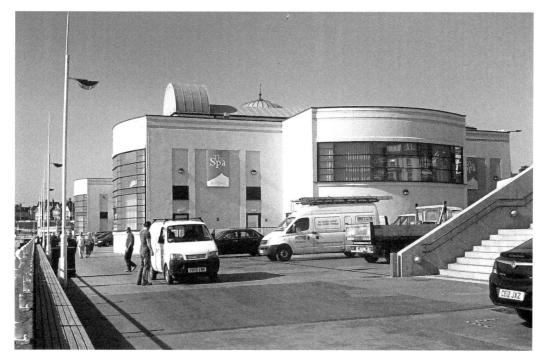

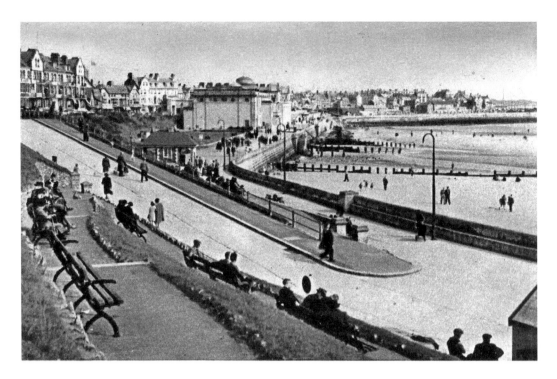

East Yorkshire Yacht Club

A general view of South Bay Promenade and beach and, below, the Royal Yorkshire Yacht Club building on the opposite side of the road, to the back of New Spa. The art deco building complements the larger spa building and gives the location a 1930s feel.

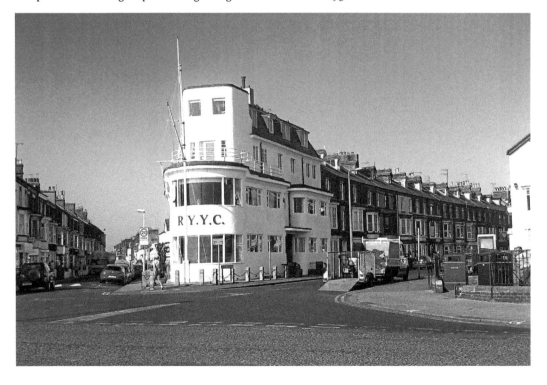

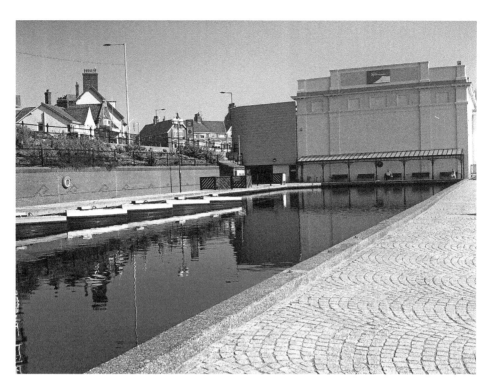

Fun and Games
The boating pool, which is next to New Spa on the south side. The children's fairground, which is next to it, is seen here in March 2012, amid preparations for the coming season.

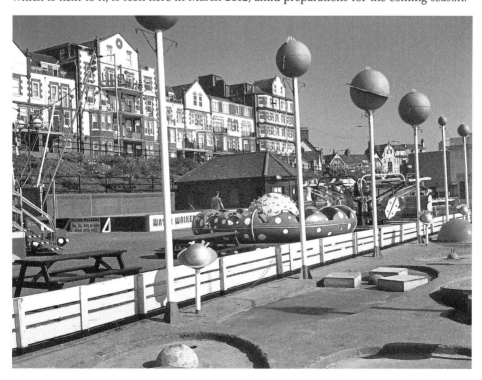

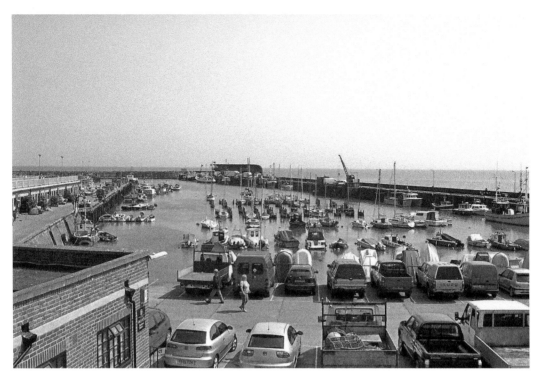

Lifeboat Station

Above are the harbour and marina in May 2006. Below is the Lifeboat Station, which is situated opposite the spa in South Marine Parade. The Lifeboat Station was established here in 1806.

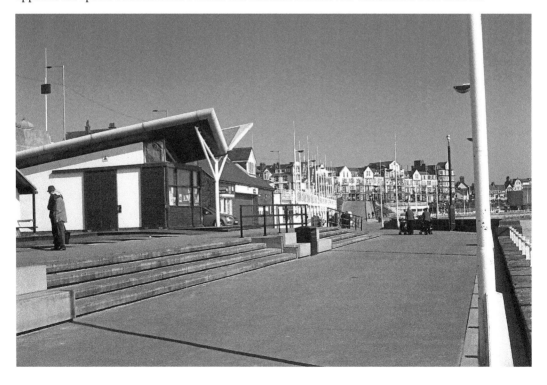

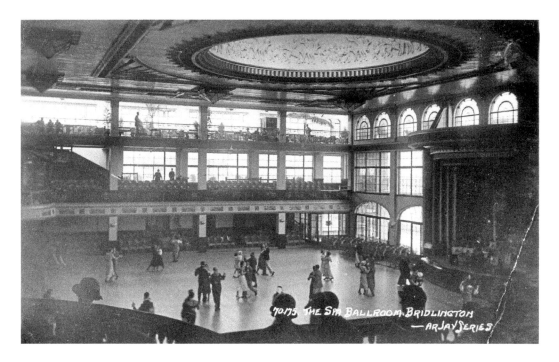

Tea Dances and the Solarium

The interior of the New Spa building, probably in the 1920s judging by the fashions on display. The top view shows the large ballroom, with what is perhaps a tea dance in progress. Such dances here have long been popular. The lower view shows the solarium, which tried to create a warm desert island feel, with palm trees among the basket-weave tables and chairs. The solarium would have been well patronised whenever the summer weather turned cold and wet.

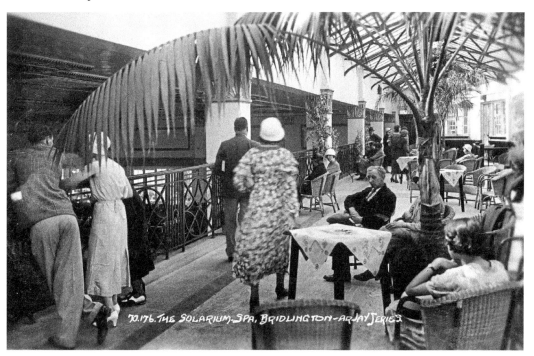

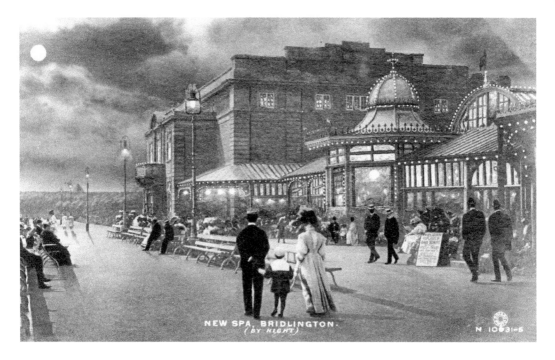

Evenings on the Promenades

The Promenades at Bridlington during early twentieth-century summer evenings. The upper view shows New Spa fully illuminated, the Promenade remaining busy. The lower view shows Prince's Parade, on the north side, illuminated by the moon. Again there are still visitors on the Promenade, although the gardens are in total darkness except for the dim Promenade lighting. The hotels and entertainments are fully lit and offer a contrast to the dark gardens.

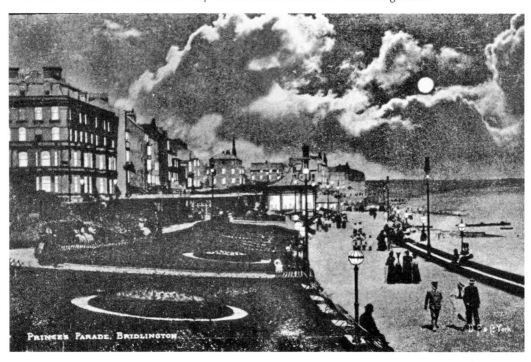

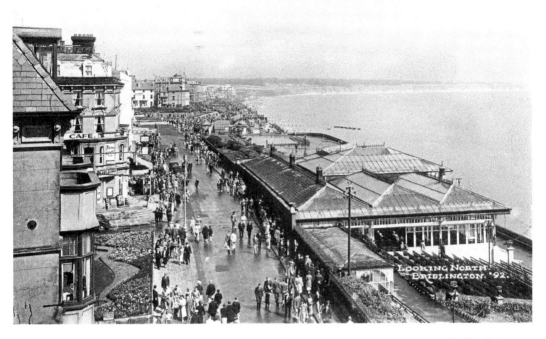

The Esplanade

Two views of the Esplanade in the early twentieth century. The views here show just how popular Bridlington was at that time.

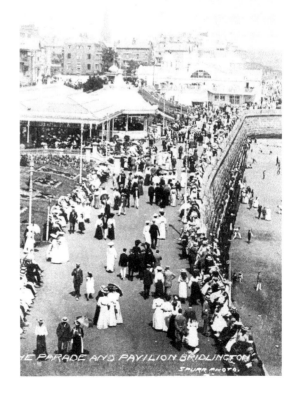

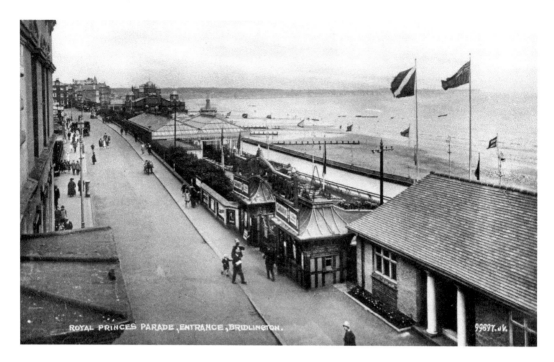

ROYAL PRINCES PARADE, ENTRANCE, BRIDLINGTON.

99897.0 V.

Royal Prince's Parade

The upper view shows Royal Prince's Parade on a wet and windy day. Royal Prince's Parade introduced a new era for the Quay and was once rather aristocratic with its floral pavilion and gardens, which included flower beds and a floral clock. In those days, the well-to-do came to take the sea air, away from the smokey towns and cities of the West Riding. The lower view shows Beaconsfield Gardens in the 1950s. The gardens are still here, but the floral displays are no more.

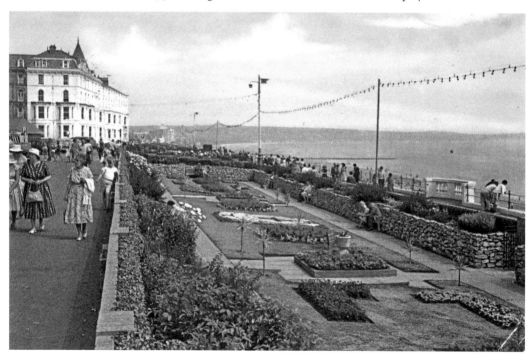

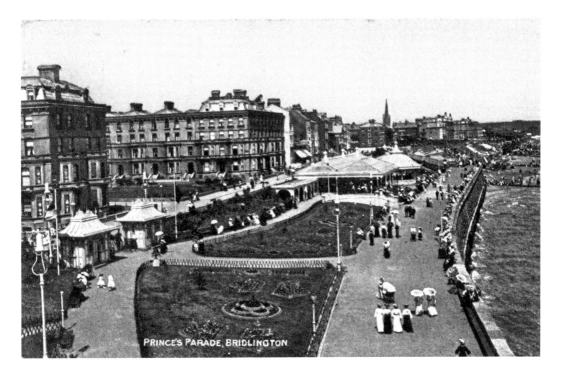

The Grand Pavilion

Prince's Parade, Bridlington, during the Edwardian period. Extensions were made here between 1904 and 1906. At that time, the Grand Pavillion was built and opened in 1906; it can be seen in the lower view. The Grand Pavillion survived for thirty years, being demolished in 1936. The colourful garden displays can also be seen here.

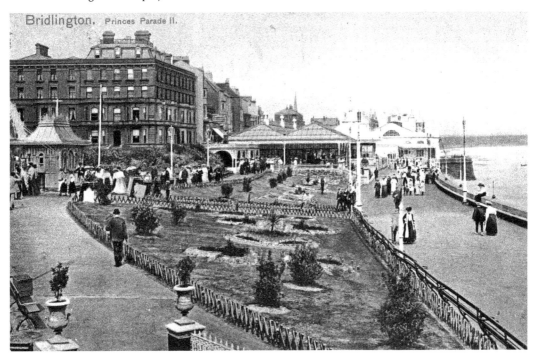

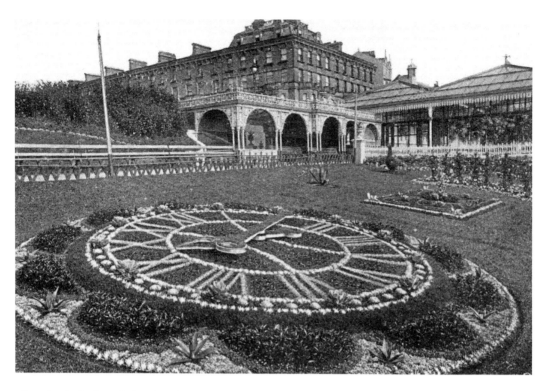

The Floral Clock and Floral Hall

The floral clock on Royal Prince's Parade, with the Floral Hall in the background. As times changed and other pleasures were sought, the floral clock was removed and sent to Sewerby Hall.

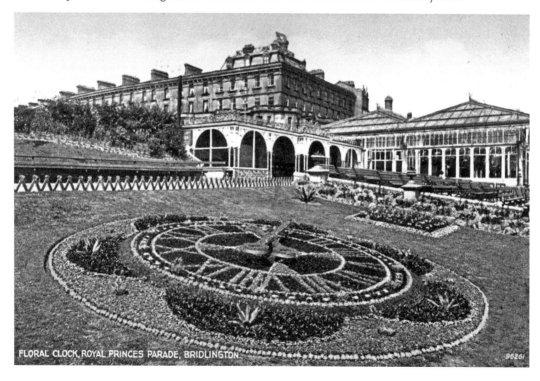

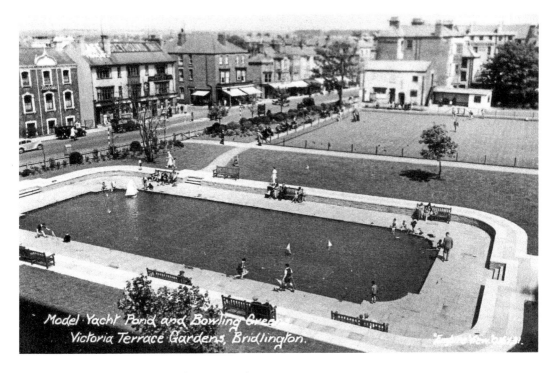

Model Yacht Pond and Bowling Greens, Victoria Terrace Gardens, Bridlington.

Victoria Terrace and North Promenade
Victoria Terrace and boating pool in the 1950s. Below is the children's pool on the North Promenade during the 1960s.

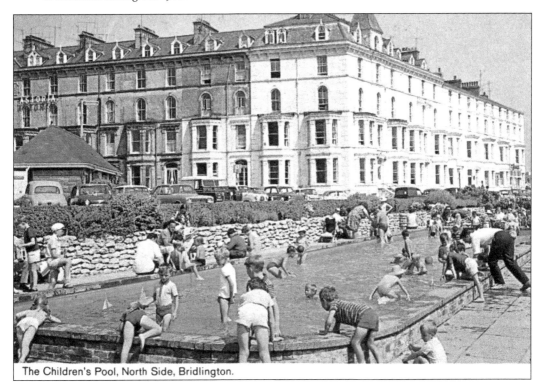

The Children's Pool, North Side, Bridlington.

59

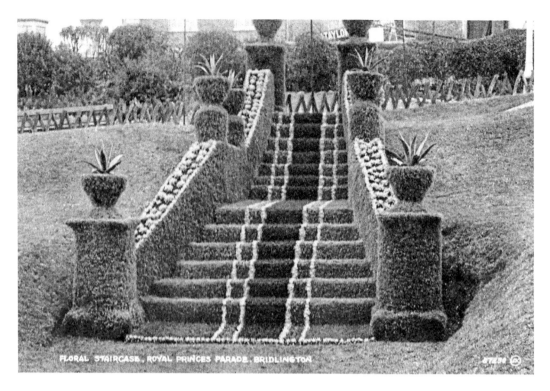

Floral Staircase and Floral Carpet

The upper view shows the floral staircase on Royal Prince's Parade during the Edwardian period, while the lower picture shows the floral carpet near the Floral Hall. It must have involved some considerable work to have achieved such structures in flowers.

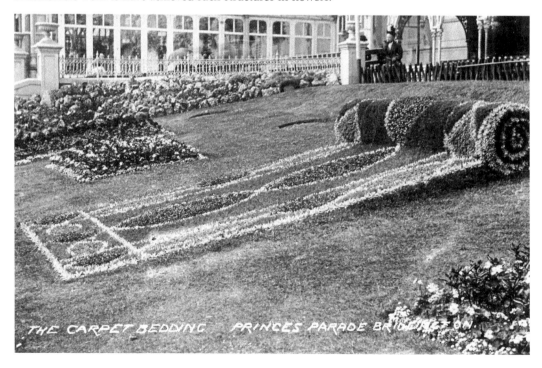

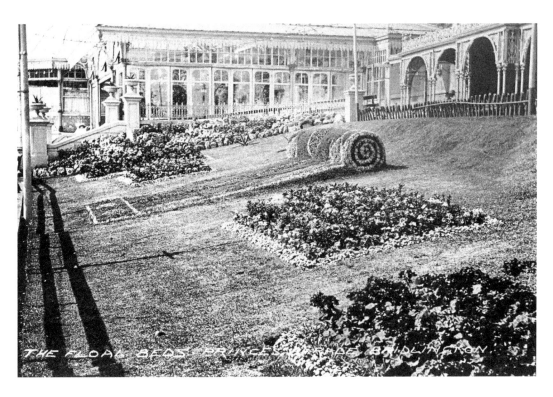

Floral Hall

Another view of the floral carpet and the exterior of the Floral Hall. The lower view is of the interior of the Floral Hall with its exotic vines and plants. The Floral Hall has long since been demolished.

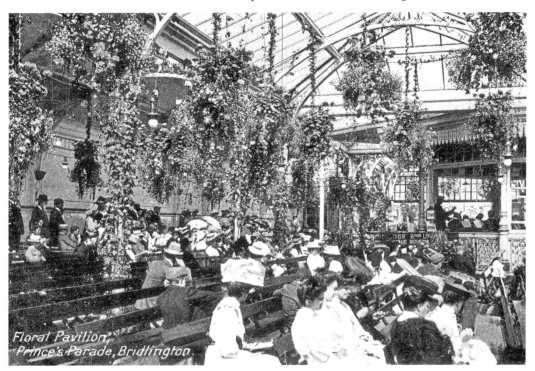

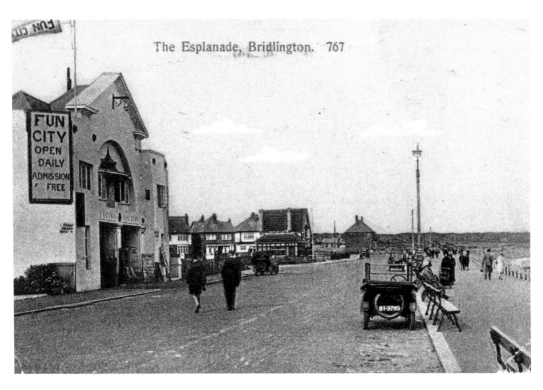

The Esplanade, Bridlington. 767

North Side

Two views from the North Side Promenade. The top view shows North Marine Drive, while the lower view shows the north side floral gardens in the 1950s.

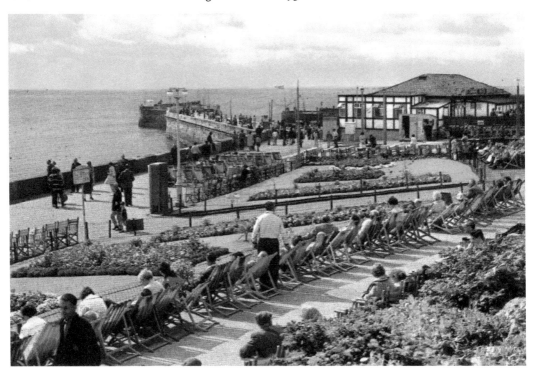

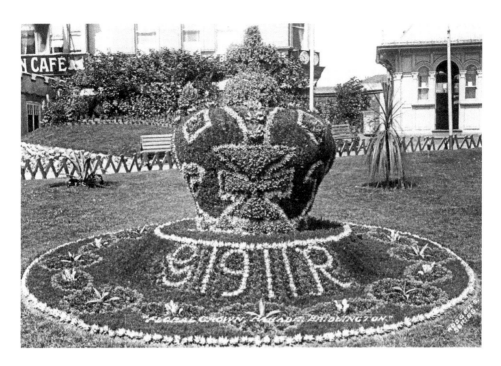

The Floral Crown
The floral crown on Prince's Parade, commemorating the coronation of King George V in 1911. The lower view shows Prince's Parade over 100 years later, with its bars and cafés on the left and a wall separating the road from the fairground, which has covered much of the old floral gardens.

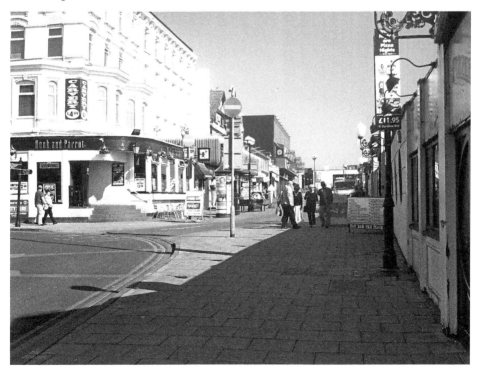

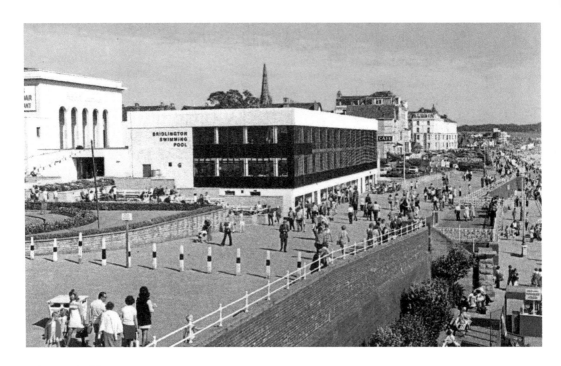

Leisure World

Standing on the former site of both a fort and the Grand Pavillion is Leisure World, which opened on 3 April 1987. The upper view shows Leisure World when newly opened, while the lower view shows it as it appears today. The local press have suggested that Leisure World may well be updated in the near future.

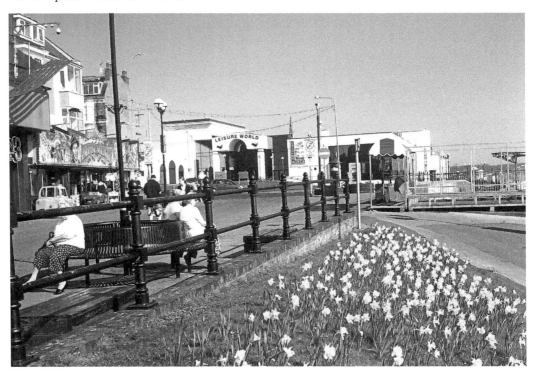

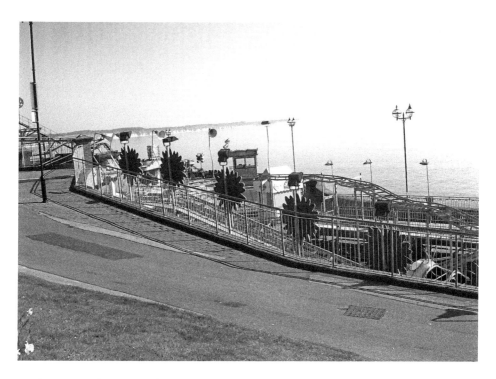

Modern Day Prince's Parade

Two views of Prince's Parade in March 2012. The area around Prince's Parade is close to the town itself and accordingly is busier than the south side. However, the seafront is no longer the exclusive location that it once was, and many of its more lavish features have gone.

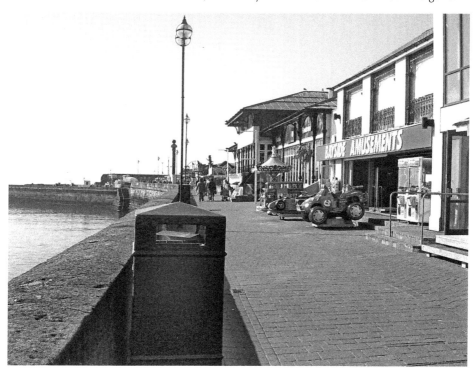

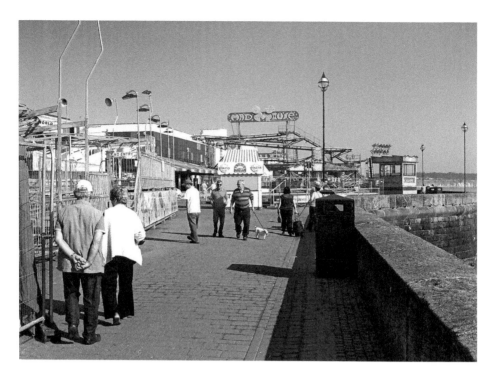

Fairground

The exclusive structures that were once on the North Promenade have been replaced by a fairground, seen here in March 2012. The owners are preparing rides and booths ready for the summer season after a long winter. At the height of the season the fairground will be busy with holidaymakers and daytrippers.

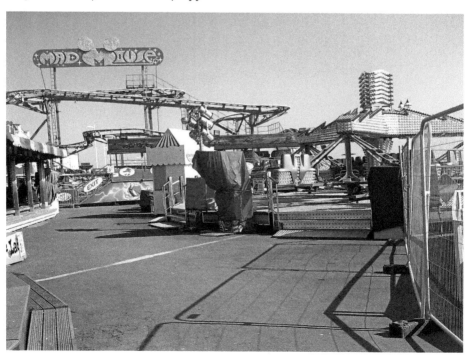

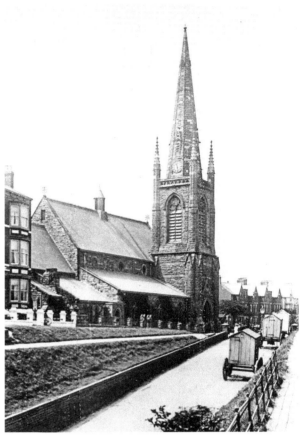

Trinity Cut and Church
At the Beaconsfield end of the north Promenade is Trinity Cut, seen here in the early twentieth century and below in 2012 with Trinity Church in the background.

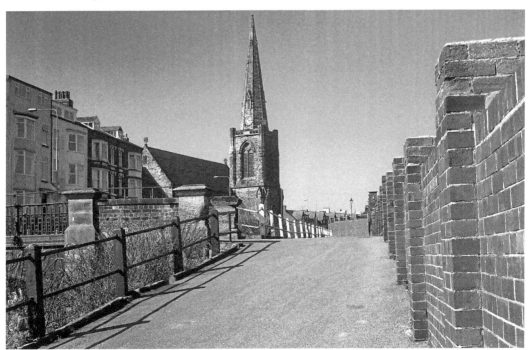

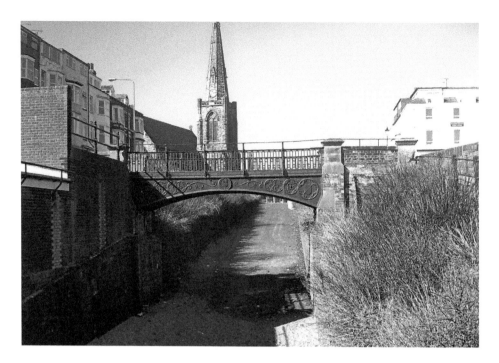

Donkey Bridge

The upper view shows the iron bridge that crosses Trinity Cut. It is known locally as 'Donkey Bridge', because this is the route by which the beach donkeys are brought down in the morning and taken home at night. Donkey Bridge is also known as the place where many a courtship has been cemented. The view below features Royal Prince's Parade in 2012. It still has the appearance of being rather elite and contains hotels and apartments. The location is quiet, away from the bustle of the town centre.

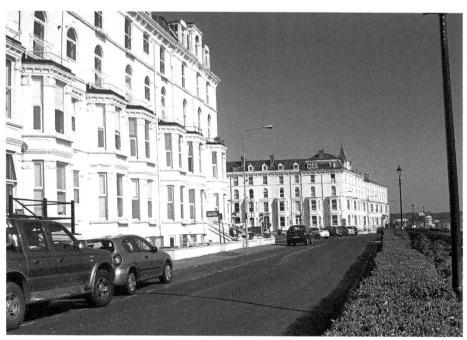

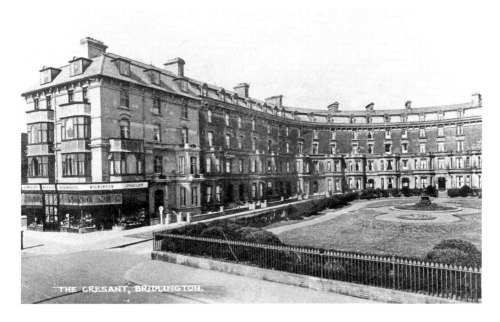

THE CRESANT, BRIDLINGTON.

Two Bridlington Crescents

The upper view shows Marlborough Terrace in the early twentieth century. It was built in 1888, along with The Crescent, seen in the 2012 view below. The Crescent appears to have fallen on hard times, with many of the apartments boarded up and the whole street looking rather dilapidated.

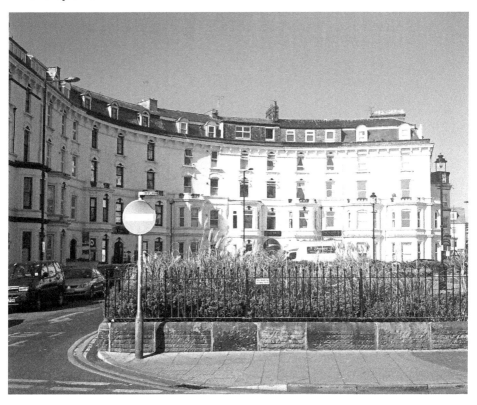

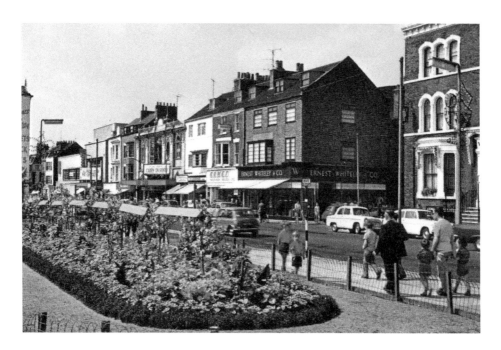

The Promenade and King Street

The Promenade, the main shopping street in Bridlington, as it appeared in 1971. The townscape at the Quay is a mixture of modern buildings. They were mostly constructed from east Yorkshire brick, due to a shortage of good building stone. Bridlington was one of the first areas in England to use bricks made from local clays. The lower view shows the corner of King Street. This road dates back to the 1800s, when a market was established on the site. It later extended to Prince Street, but is now solely on King Street once again.

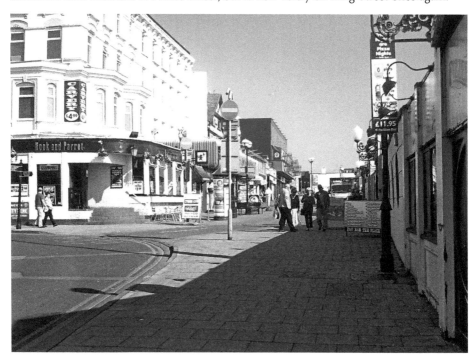

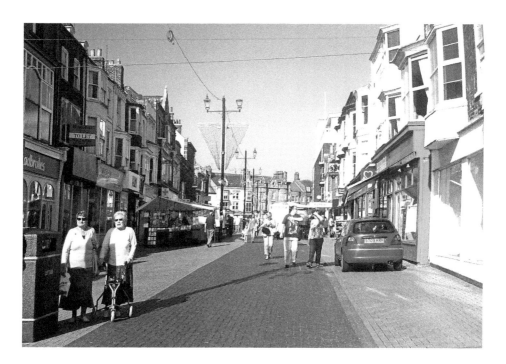

Chapel Street

Chapel Street in March 2012, just outside the Promenades shopping centre; an entrance to the shopping centre from the bus station can be seen in the lower view. The Promenades was built on the site of a demolished church about ten years ago. For a while after the church had been demolished the organ remained *in situ*, exposed to the elements, until it was removed.

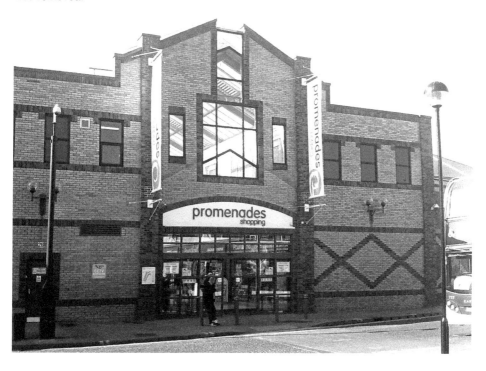

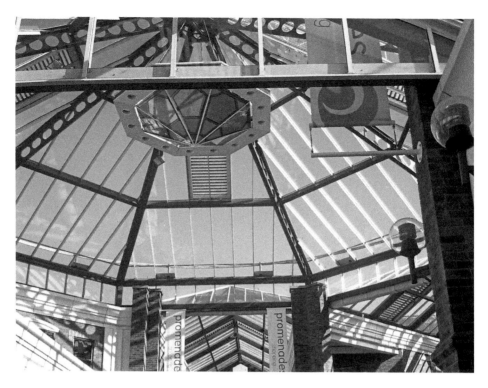

The Promenades Shopping Centre
Interior views of the Promenades shopping centre, showing the glass dome in the centre and one of the aisles radiating from it, with shops on both sides.

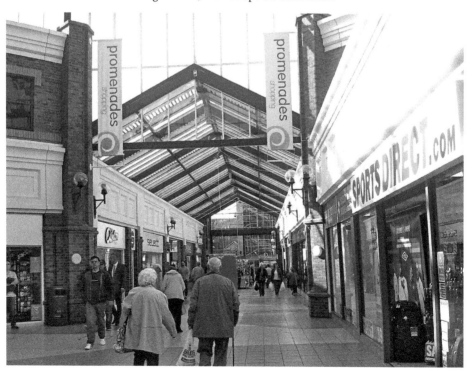

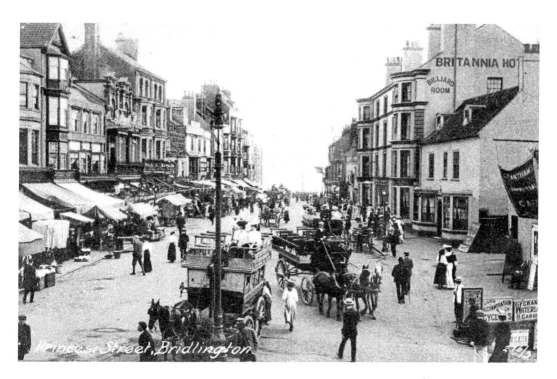

Prince's Street

Two views of Prince's Street in the early twentieth century. The postcard actually says that this is King Street, but that is incorrect. Before the Quay was starting to develop as a resort it was very small and had only 120 houses in 1672, compared with 232 in Old Town. By 1808 the population on the Quay was still only 687, while there were 3,130 residents in Old Town.

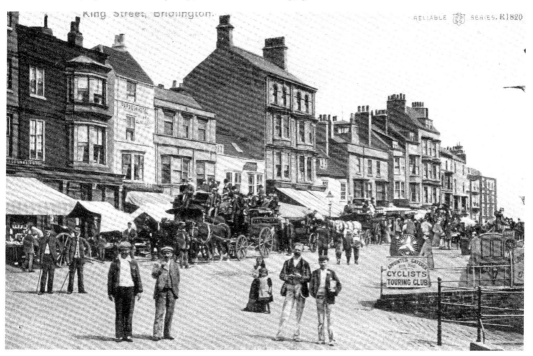

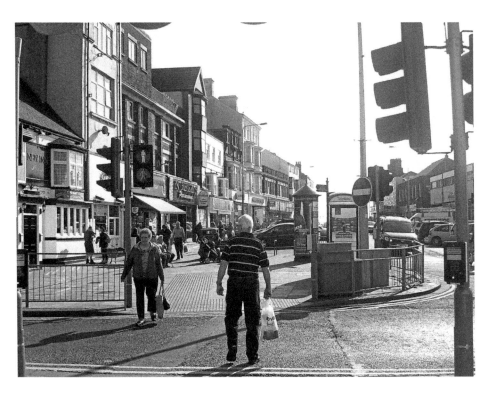

Modern Town Centre
Bridlington town centre in March 2012, showing the Promenade and Queen Street.

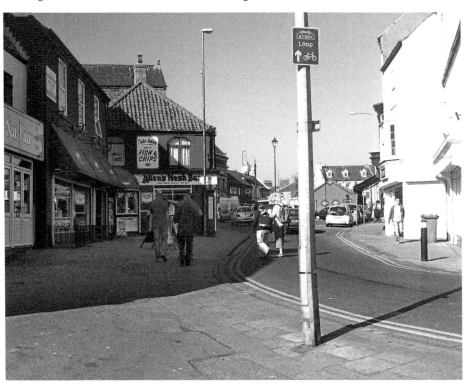

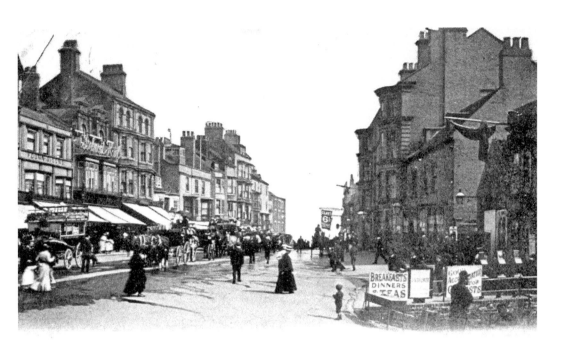

Changing Times

The top view shows Prince's Street during the Edwardian period, while the lower view shows the Promenade in 2012. It is evident just how much the town has changed over the years.

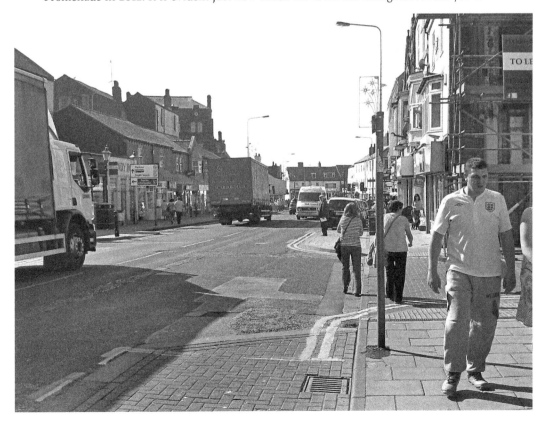

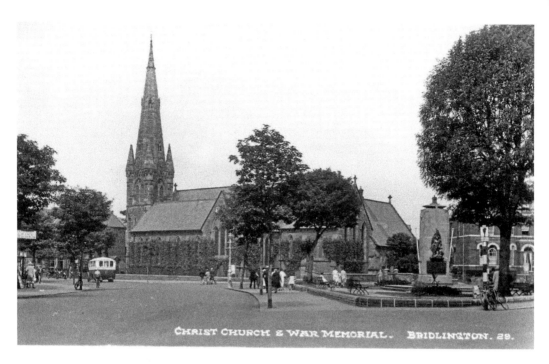

Christ Church

Christ church was built in 1840. The upper view shows the church with the war memorial in the 1930s, and the lower view shows Christ church in March 2012.

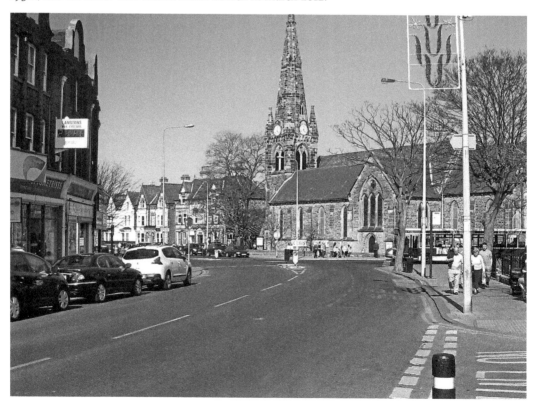

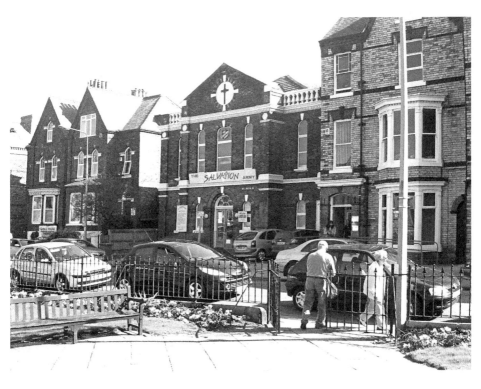

War Memorial

Surrounding the war memorial garden is the Salvation Army citadel, seen above in March 2012, and below is the war memorial itself.

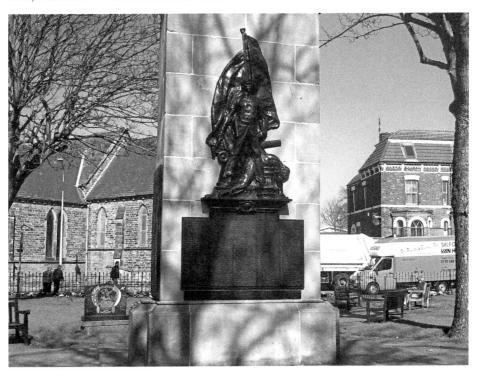

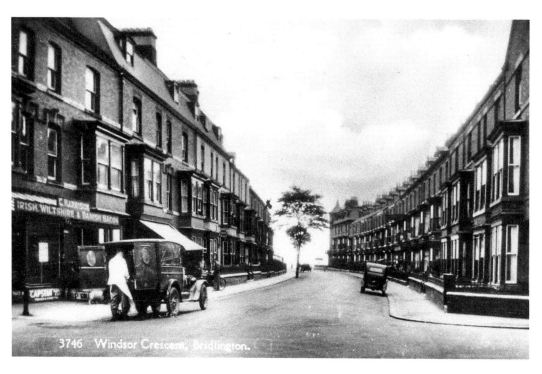

Windsor Crescent and Quay Road

The upper view shows Windsor Crescent in the 1940s, while the lower view is of Quay Road, which links the Quay with Old Town. This early twentieth-century view is looking south.

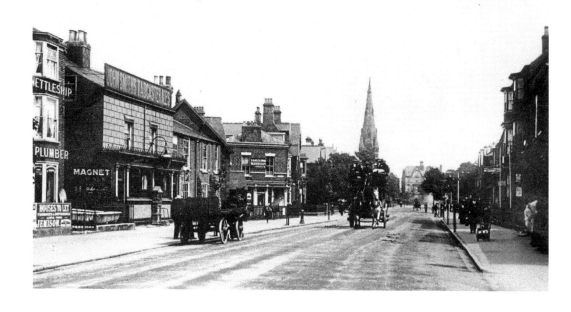

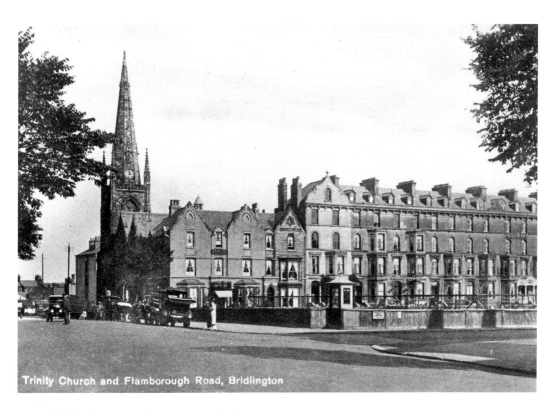

Trinity Church and Flamborough Road, Bridlington

Trinity Church and Lansdowne Road

In the upper view we see Trinity church, looking towards the Promenade. The lower picture is of Lansdowne Road, with its large houses in the 1950s. They are now mostly guest houses or flats.

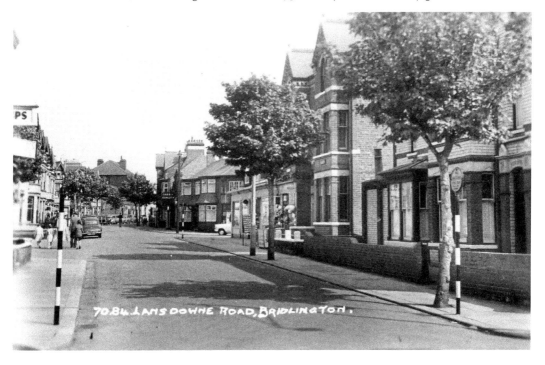

70.84 LANSDOWNE ROAD, BRIDLINGTON.

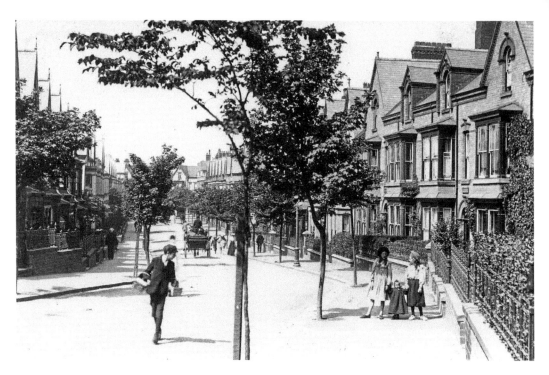

Tennyson Avenue and Flamborough Road

Two more local roads in Bridlington. The upper picture is of Tennyson Avenue with its substantial properties, which was formerly known as Jemmy Tenny Lane. Below is Flamborough Road. The biggest expansion of Bridlington came between 1881 and 1901, with considerable building in the Hilderthorpe area. Between 1891 and 1901 the whole population of the town grew from 6,840 to 12,482.

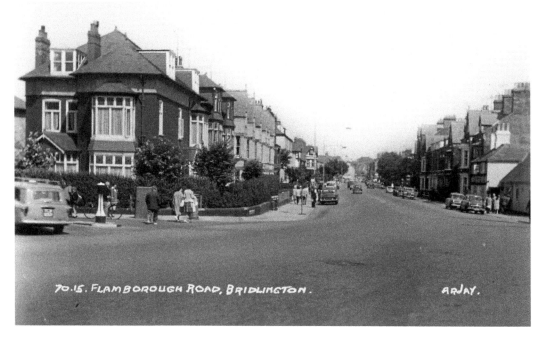

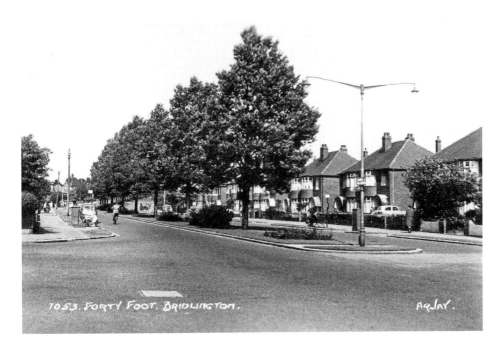

Fortyfoot

Fortyfoot in the 1950s and 2012. Fortyfoot links the outer part of Bridlington, close to Sewerby, with the Quay. It was built in 1299. At 40 feet wide, it was a very wide road for the period, built specifically for the ease of delivering goods to the harbour. The road was financed by Sir William St Quinten. The upper view shows that Fortyfoot has become a dual carriageway by the 1950s, with trees in the middle. Today, the trees have been removed.

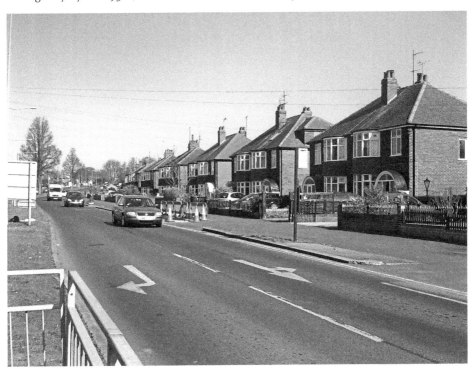

81

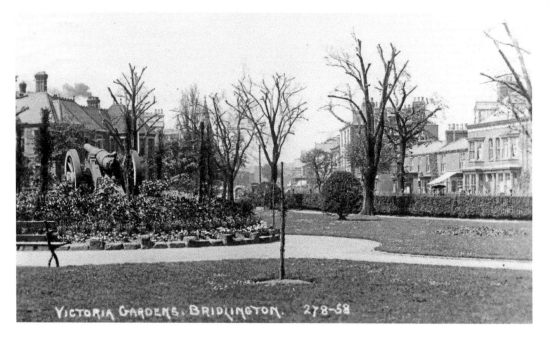

Victoria Gardens, Bridlington. 278-58

Bridlington at War

Above is a view of Victoria Gardens in the 1930s, with its display of flowers and shrubbery, topped by a cannon Below is St Anne's convalescent home before the outbreak of the First World War. During the Second World War, the home was hit by German bombs and was destroyed. Retirement bungalows are now on the site. Houses on Hilderthorpe Road were also destroyed by enemy bombs during the war; the aircraft were probably jettisoning their loads before heading back out over the North Sea.

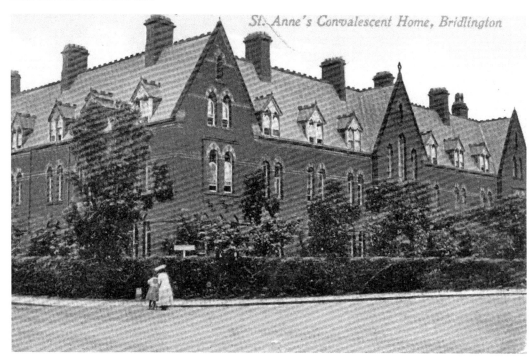

St. Anne's Convalescent Home, Bridlington

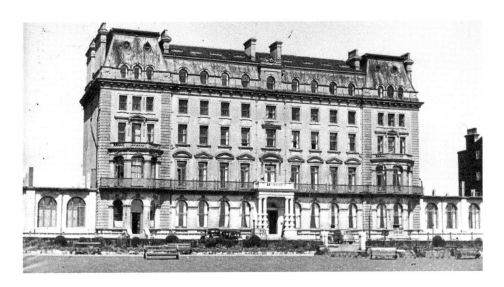

Catering for the Holidaymakers

The Alexandra Hotel was an impressive building that once housed the well-to-do who stayed in the town for their holidays. It was built between 1863 and 1866, but has since been demolished. Other structures built for the holidaymakers were the Victoria Rooms on the north pier, which was built in 1846 and burnt down in 1933 and the Hydro, on South Marine Drive, built in 1898. Along with the railway, public transport was provided in Bridlington. By the end of the nineteenth century Williamson's operated a horse bus service, which can be seen in this view. The stables for the horses were at a site on Havelock Crescent, now a garage.

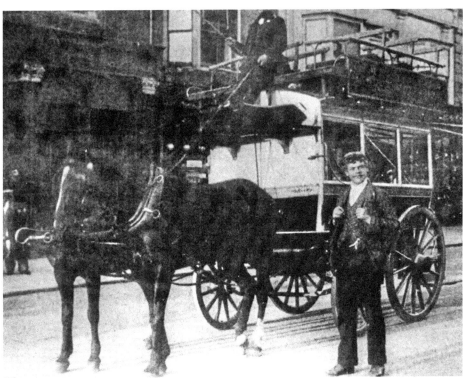

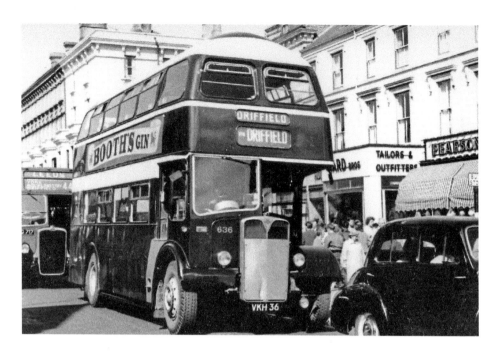

Bus Services

Since 1926, bus services in Bridlington have been operated by East Yorkshire Motor Services, their vehicles being painted in dark blue livery with cream bands, as can be seen in this view of AEC Regent III double-decker bus on the Promenade. EYMS usually ran Leyland vehicles, an example of which can be seen behind destined for Leeds. The AEC has a Beverley bar roof, to fit under the low arches in the town walls at Beverley. It is now part of the EYMS heritage fleet. In 1969 EYMS was taken over by the National Bus Company and, after 1972, corporate poppy red was used on the vehicles, as can be seen on this AEC Regent V, shown on Cross Street.

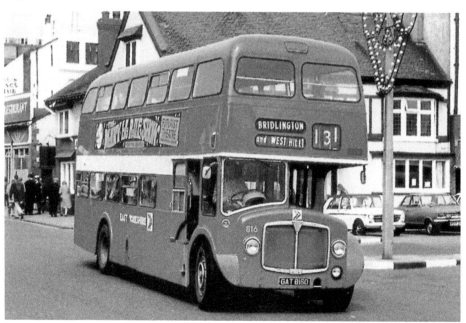

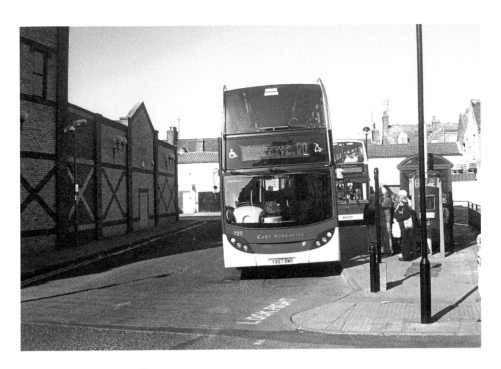

Buses and Sewerby Hall

In 1987, EYMS was bought out by its management and its buses were then painted in the current livery of maroon and cream, an example of which can be seen in this modern image, from the bus station behind the Promenades shopping centre. The bus is a Volvo Olympian and it is on the 120 service from Bridlington to Scarborough, via the holiday camps. Just a mile north-east of Bridlington is the village of Sewerby, famous for the tourist attraction of Sewerby Hall, a Grade I listed building and home to the Museum of East Yorkshire, which features a room dedicated to aviatrix Amy Johnson. The lower picture here shows an aerial view of the hall and its gardens.

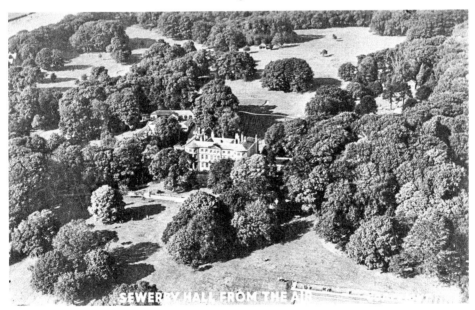

SEWERBY HALL FROM THE AIR

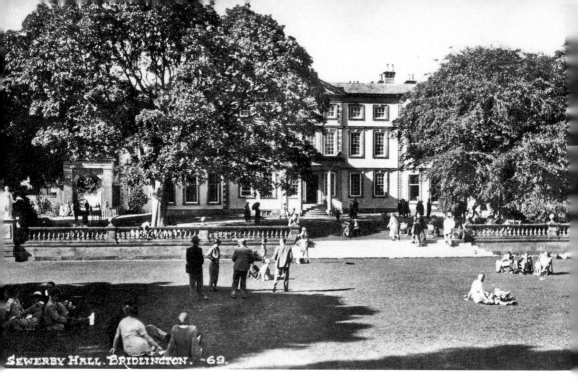

Sewerby Hall and Park

Sewerby Hall in the 1950s. The hall was built on a Tudor site between 1714 and 1720 by the Graeme family. It was acquired by Bridlington Corporation in 1934 and opened to the public two years later. It was Amy Johnson who performed the opening ceremony on that day. Below is a bandstand in Sewerby Park.

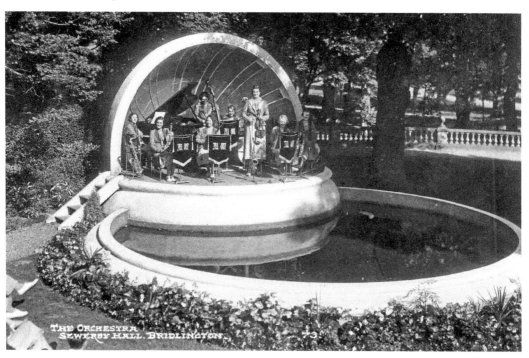

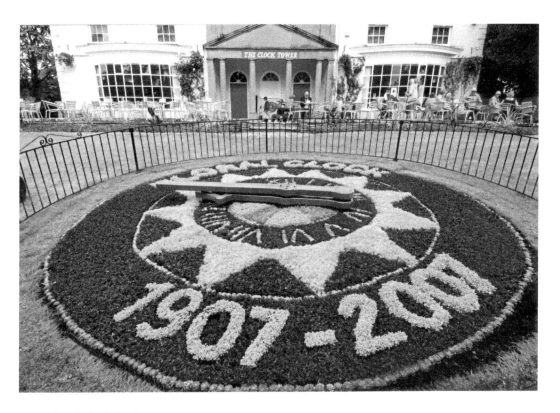

Floral Clock Centenary

The upper view shows the floral clock at Sewerby Hall on the occasion of its centenary in 2007. The lower view shows the Old English Gardens at Sewerby Park.

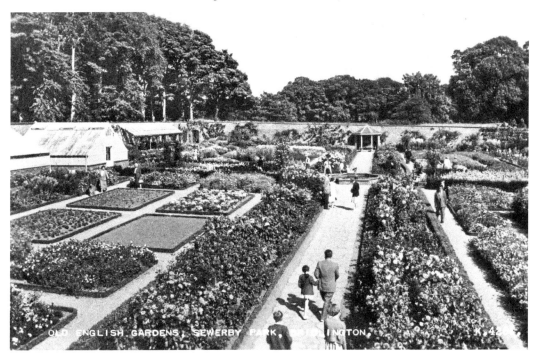

OLD ENGLISH GARDENS, SEWERBY PARK, BRIDLINGTON.

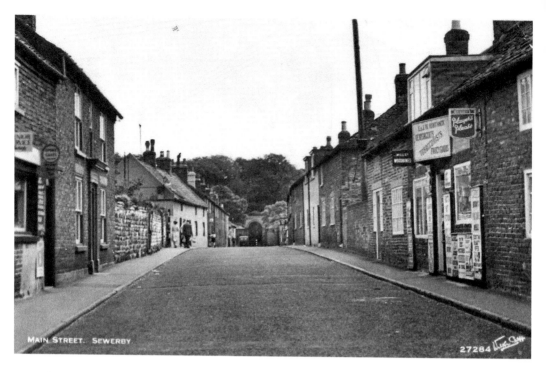

Sewerby Village

Two views of Sewerby village. Although rather small, it has its own church and pub. The village is situated between Bridlington and Flamborough and looks out across Bridlington Bay. It was here in 1779 that John Paul Jones took on the might of the Royal Navy during the American War of Independence, watched by crowds along the shore.

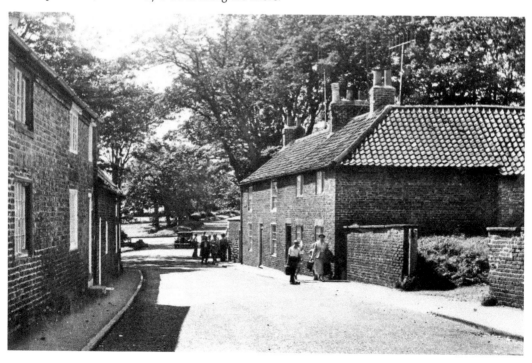

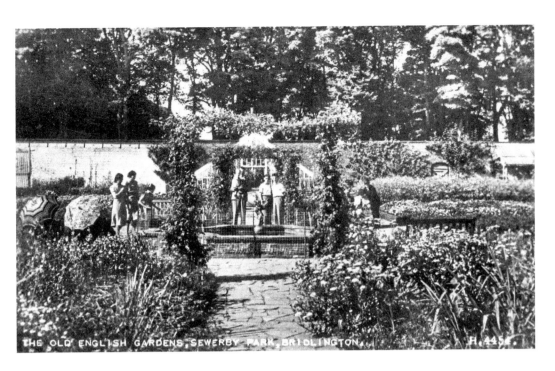

The Old English Gardens, Sewerby Park, Bridlington. H. 445.

Sewerby Hall Gardens
The upper view shows the gardens at Sewerby Hall in the 1950s, while the lower view shows Sewerby Hall in January 2012.

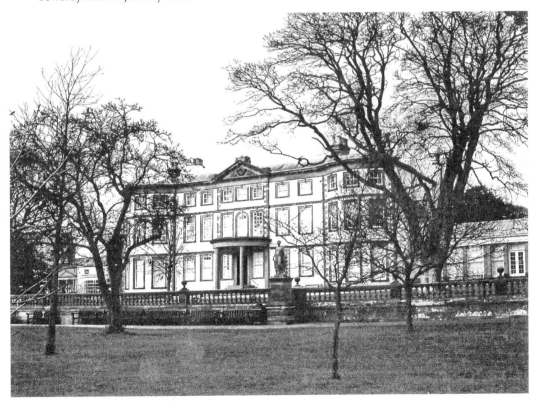

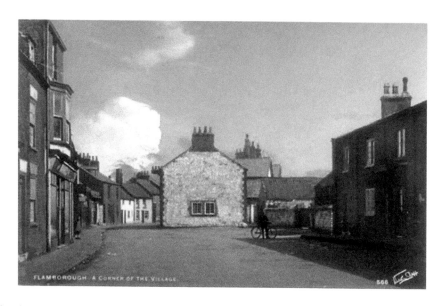

Flamborough

High Street, Flamborough, in the 1970s. The village is situated four miles east of Bridlington, on the headland that extends some six miles into the North Sea. The village has a population of around 2,000 people and is a popular holiday spot. The remains of Flamborough Castle, a medieval fortified manor house, can also be seen here. Below is the village's parish church of St Oswald.

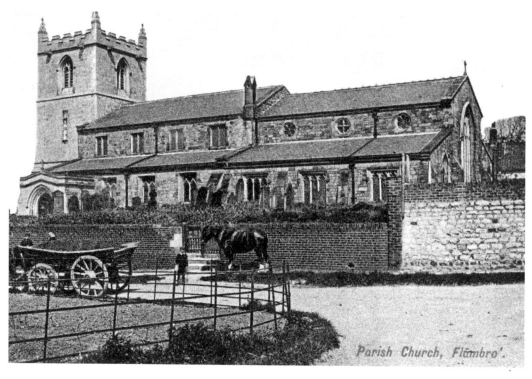

Parish Church, Flambro'.

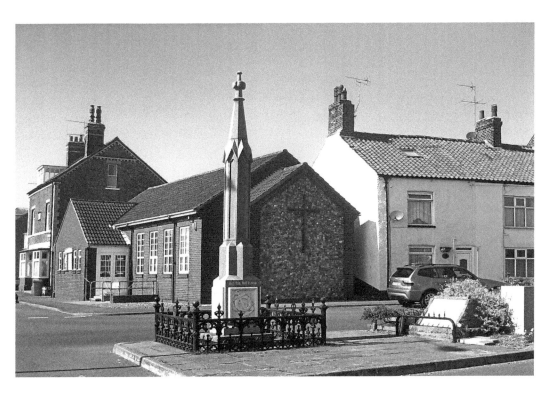

Modern Flamborough
Two views of High Street North End, Flamborough, in March 2012.

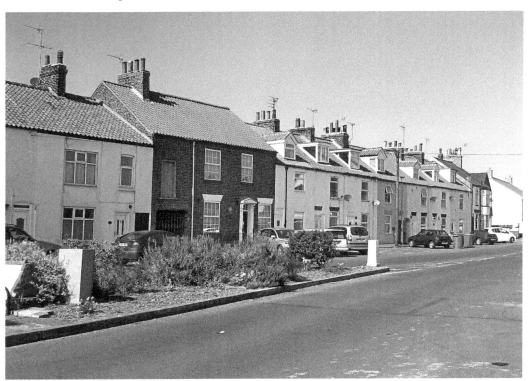

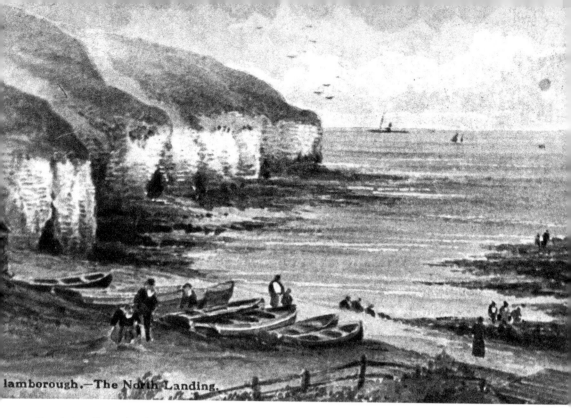

lamborough.—The North Landing.

North Landing, Flamborough.
The upper view shows the North Landing in the eighteenth century, with the little rowing boats used here for fishing. Beyond are the chalk cliffs where the Yorkshire Wolds meet the North Sea. Below is the landing in the 1970s with the lifeboat in view, essential in this area of treacherous seas.

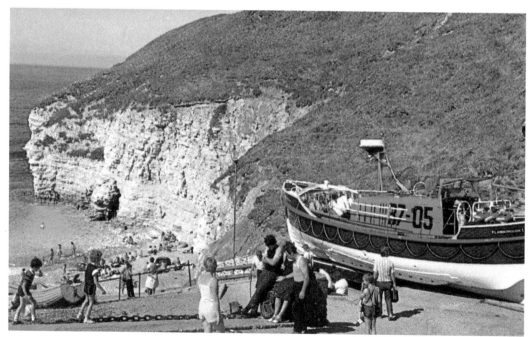

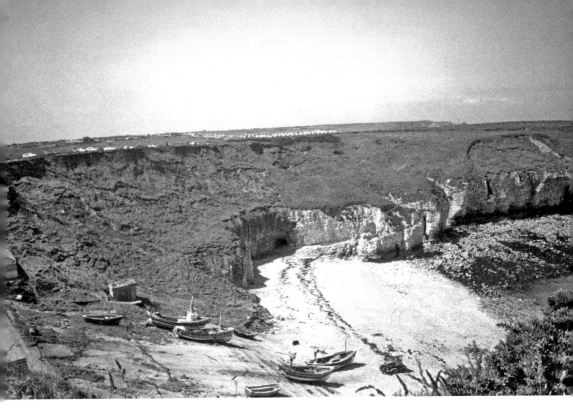

The Landings
North and South Landings at Flamborough in 2005.

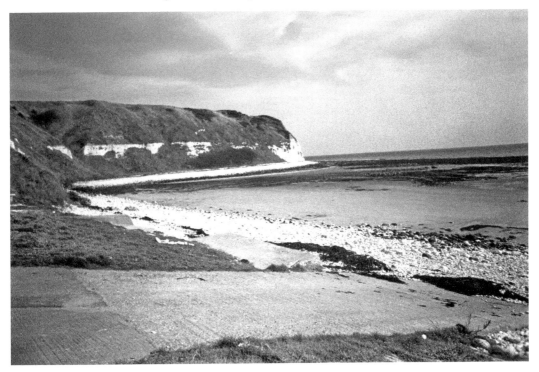

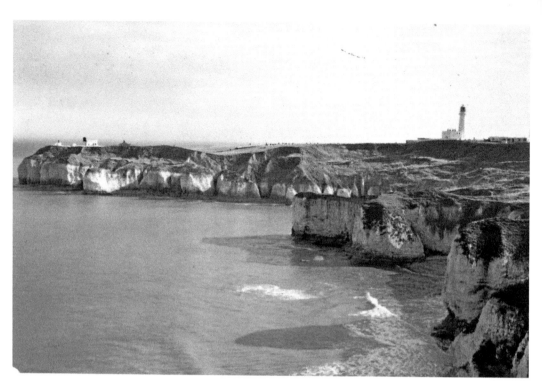

Birds

The limestone cliffs at Flamborough are filled with birds during the mating season. It is a noisy place when these birds are vying for space on the cliffs and protecting their nests.

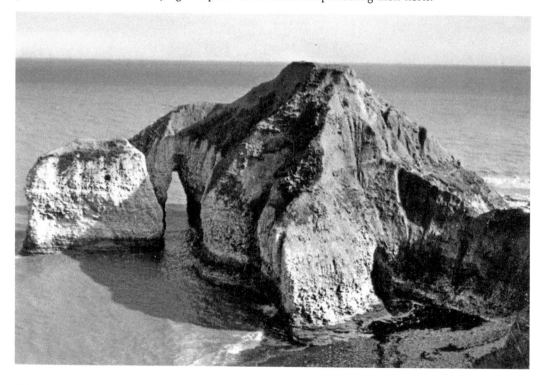

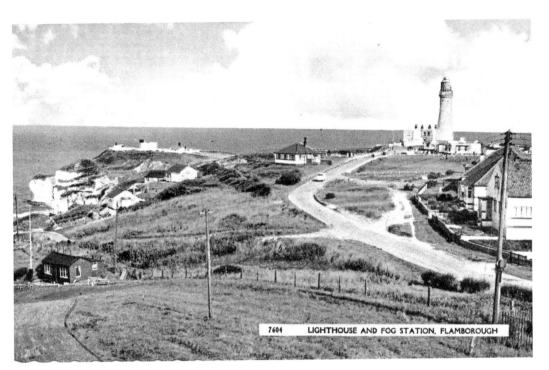

7604   LIGHTHOUSE AND FOG STATION, FLAMBOROUGH

The Lighthouse and Beacon Tower

The lighthouse seen in the upper view was built by a local customs officer in 1806 to warn of the dangers of the rocky coast at Flamborough, 174 ships having foundered off the coast in the previous thirty-six years. The lighthouse stands at 92 feet high, and has 3½ million candle power. The light is visible for some 21 miles and can be seen from as far away as Whitby and the River Humber. The original lighthouse, in the lower view, is believed to have been built in 1673 with the approval of Charles II, who also gave permission to collect dues from passing ships. The Beacon Tower was probably not a lighthouse as such, but a beacon designed to warn of a forthcoming invasion.

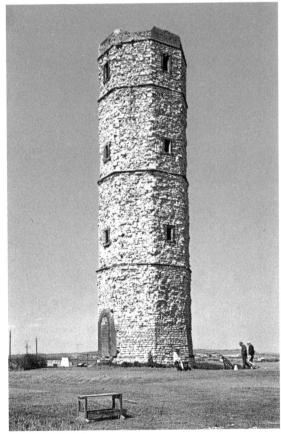

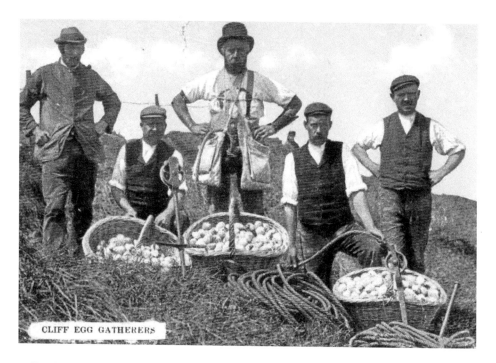

CLIFF EGG GATHERERS

Collecting Gull Eggs

A source of employment for some of the population of Flamborough was the collection of gull eggs from the cliff faces. It was a dangerous job, which involved hanging off a rope to take the eggs from the cliffs. The birds would often attack to protect their eggs, and seagulls can be very aggressive creatures. A group of men engaged in this task are seen here. The practice died out in later years. Whatever the rights or wrongs of the custom, it certainly kept the number of seagulls in check, whereas now we are overrun with them!

Acknowledgements

I have had a lot of fun putting this book together and have learnt much about Bridlington and its surroundings from the local people that I met while working on the project.

I would like to thank the many people who helped, in particular Derek Wilson, who kindly supplied pictures and even took the time to put them onto disc for me. I would also like to thank Tina Pickering for her assistance in finding out about the history of Old Town and taking the trouble to show me around. Thanks also go to Rebekah Walkington and Franco Villani for their contributions to the history of the hospitals in Bridlington. Further thanks go to Judith Lea, Bernard Unsworth, Jennie Sharp, John Thurston, June Seggin, Ellen Morris and Richard Casserley for their contributions.

I apologise for any omissions I may have made, but I hope that I have used the information well and that as much pleasure is derived from reading this book as I had in writing it.

Finally, my thanks go to Hilary for her constant support and supplies of tea while I was beavering away.